Surya Susan Bijoy

A Journalist by profession who has experience in Print, Radio, TV and Internet media forms from the last 2 decades. At present she is a passionate Toastmaster who has won the Golden Quill Award for the Best Writer from District 105, of Toastmasters International which was the solo selection from 5 countries. She supports Toastmasters International in various ways as a Champion Speaker, Judge for Contests and a Club Coach. She has held the position of President, Vice President Public Relations and Secretary in various Toastmasters clubs in U.A.E. and helped in Newsletter works for the Toastmasters clubs in Doha and Dubai.

Surya Bijoy is the President of the Ladies Wing of Indira Gandhi Veekshanam Forum in Sharjah and works for social causes in various fields.

At the personal front she is happily married to Bijoy Pothen Manathara who is a senior Engineer working with the Jacobs company in Dubai. She is blessed with a son Cyril Bijoy and daughter Karen Mariam Bijoy, both are studying in school at present. Born and raised in Delhi, and at present settled in Dubai, Surya is a happy professional and a sweet homemaker.

PH: 00971555665877
email: suryabijoy@gmail.com

English Language
Surya Rise and Shine
(Essays)
by
Surya Susan Bijoy

Published in November 2023
by Decan Imprint Publishing Co.
Reg. Off: Sharjah Publishing City
Free Zone Sharjah, UAE.
Phone: 00971-551830334
Email : decanimprint@gmail.com

Cover Design : Karen Mariam Bijoy

Printed at
Printing Park, Tly.

11/23-24/Sl.No.11/250/NS 18.6
ISBN 978-93-5973-855-0

Surya Rise and Shine

Surya Susan Bijoy

DECANIMPRINT

Dedicated to my beloved parents who are my Guardian Angels. My father Dr. George Varghese who was a renowned Journalist in Delhi. My mother Mrs. Sosamma Varghese was a Teacher and a Freelance Journalist. Both my parents encouraged and supported me very strongly and lovingly especially in fulfilling all my endeavors in my life. My first book is my humble tribute to them as a daughter.

I would like to thank my husband Bijoy Pothen Manathara. He made me the Editor of both our official pages especially The Sun Times and he supported me strongly to help me continue my journalism career when we settled in the U.A.E, 10 years ago. We were in Doha, Qatar before we came to U.A.E in 2012. I would like to thank Ismail Meladi who has supported me like my own brother to bring out my first book in the Sharjah International Book fair in the year 2023. I would like to thank my children Cyril Bijoy and Karen Mariam Bijoy for encouraging and supporting me in all my endevours in life. I would like to thank my family, friends, and Toastmasters Fraternity and all my well wishers whose strong support and positive encouragement makes me feel sweetly successful always.

Preface or Introduction

Surya Rise and Shine is my first book in which I have compiled 107 articles or blogs which I wrote as an Editor for my Official Facebook Page called Sun Times. My husband Bijoy Pothen Manathara helped me start this Sun Times FB Page after we shifted to Dubai in 2013. He has designed the cover page and has contributed to its content by sharing his articles too. But in this Book I have excluded them as I will be adding those in my next book. Sun Times is a page which focuses on posting only positive and motivational theme based posts. My blogs are my way of spreading optimism and hope to all my readers...

Readers will get a dose of positivity and motivation with a dash of entertainment by being a part of Sun Times page.

Are you what you think or are you what you eat?

I know you must be in a conflict situation to answer this simple question today. Whenever you want to answer this question in today's stressful times you will not be able to choose happily between these 2 conditions.

We all are bombarded with a huge load of opinions to find our own path or secret of happiness and peace.

But if you take things simply then you will realise that what you eat or feed your body, mind and soul really influences the way you think. The way you think either makes you and breaks you. Choice is yours!

Please feed your mind with wisdom and press the stop or pause button when your own mind says , "I am full...and this is enough for me today!"

Each day of your life is different and each day will be different depending on your mindset.

If you think you are right all the time it's easy but does it make you truly happy? What is the right thought or the right action for you might be a mistake in the eyes of your loved one be it a friend or family member or your colleagues. But if you stick to your opinion then there will be conducting a mistake. Try to take the best and learn to let go of the rest. It's like a filter to only choose pure thoughts which apply best for your peace and throwing out the rest which will poison your life!

That's the best way to face conflict situations and grow as a strong warrior in life. So please think with an open heart and without any prejudices or biased opinions or influences which could actually ruin your happiness and peace, making you regret later in life..

Please feed your mind with good faith, courage, knowledge, determination and sincerity so that you are the true winner in every challenge that life could dare to throw at you!

Start becoming truly mindful, sensible and remain as the beautiful and strong human you are right now and will be in your future. Stay happy, hopeful and blessed always.

#happiness #successmindset #peaceofmind

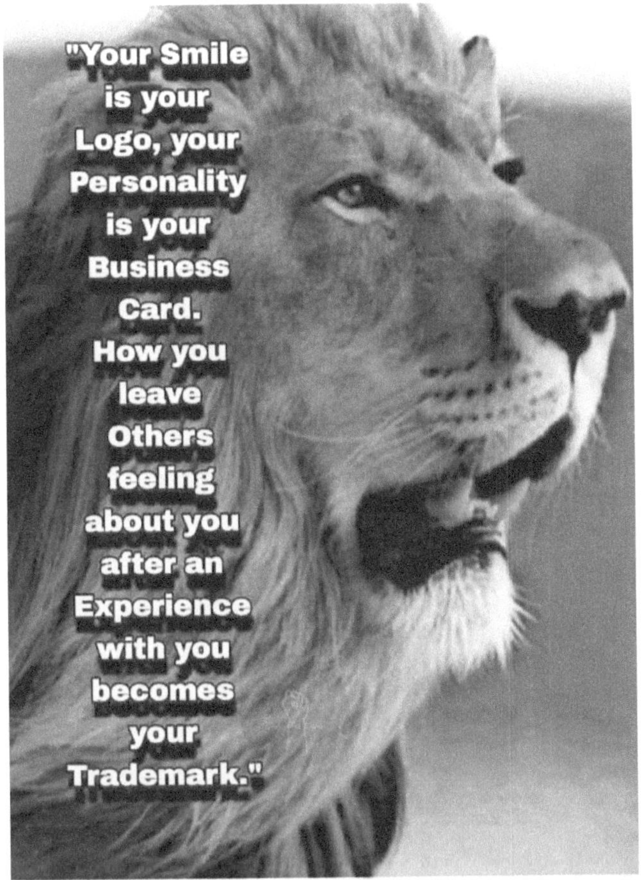

Do you meet others with a smile and try to never stop smiling to show how strong you are even when you are facing great problems in your own life? If your answer is yes then you are the Winner and Champion of life's battles already...

Yes my friend 'Fortune favours the brave' indeed. If you are brave enough to fight your life's battles with a smile of strength on your beautiful face then believe me you are the best and will be the best in all your endeavors in life. Anyone who meets you and sees you smiling will feel that you are so warm, and sweet as a person which is very important especially in these critical and stressful times.

If you really want your smile to be reflected by those you meet and to those truly matter to you be it in your personal or professional life, you have to smile. You create that sweet positivity and spread your loving grace on all your family, friends and well-wishers just by your simple smile first. So please keep smiling and spreading your peace, hope and positivity to all you meet in your life. That's the best gift you can freely give and receive freely too...and the best part it will make you so happy in the long run that you will keep smiling from deep within your soul every day of your precious life. Stay happy, blessed and please keep smiling always.

#happiness #peacebuilding #Fortune #successmindset

Are you brave enough to be alone or do you need someone to constantly be with you to push you ahead in life?

If you still are not brave enough to walk or think or take decisions alone then you are really not brave to take on the world's pressures now! Please become ready to become a true leader in your life before you lose all the time you have in your life for it.

Yes I know it's a bitter truth and if you can face it with a golden smile and become stronger then you have made your first grand step towards becoming powerful in reality.

We all are alone, as in I mean we are born as one human and we die as one human. We will face so many problems and challenges in our life till we die. But if you learn from your past mistakes and your daily life experiences you will become a strong human being and your internal wisdom will make you more confident and mature with time. Yes my friend…'Life is the biggest Teacher' and if you are ready to learn well then you will become the 'Best' in your life in whatever work you do be it personally or professionally!

So please become strong, independent and powerful in your heart, mind and your soul. You are unique and you have the power to be the best but this power is hidden deep inside your mind. You just need to work hard on making that power within you shine as bright as the sun and I assure you that you will be the happiest human being soon in your life…Please stay happy, brave and blessed always.

#brainstorming #determination
#leadershiplessons #happiness

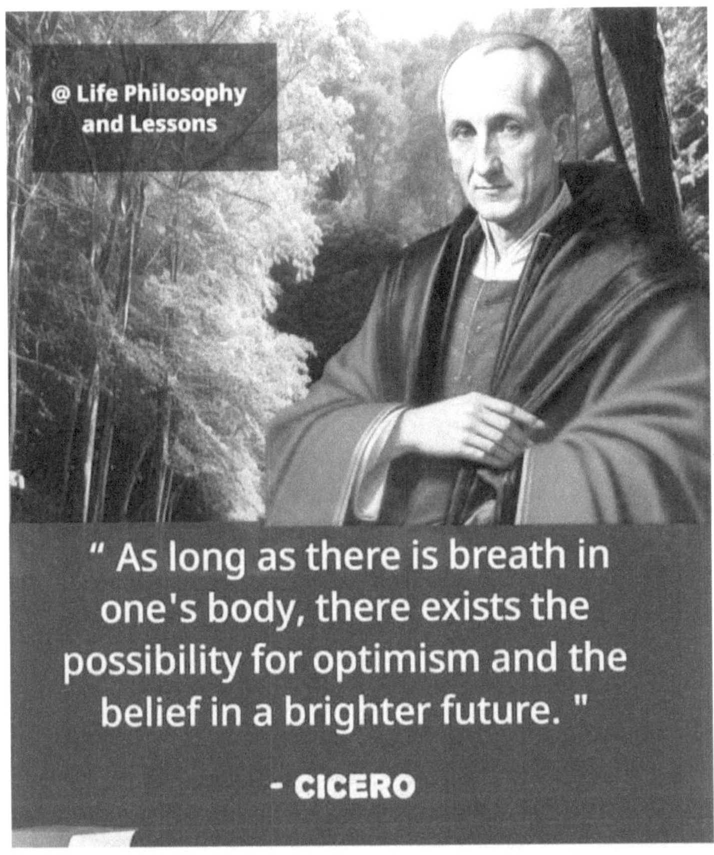

Are you ready to live with Good Hope and Leave your bitter past experiences Forever?

I hope your answer is yes to my simple question. We all have many sad life experiences but how we react and get back to a cheerful life is the Real challenge that Life loves to throw at you....

Bow to negativity and even if that's for an hour you will end up in becoming like ashes of dead bodies....But if you can live to rise and to think that you can and you will beat this devil which is standing tall in front of you to kill you and all your happiness then you will discover your hidden powers to react and beat this devil strongly in your full might!

So please rise from your sad slumber or painful sufferings to rise like the almighty Sun and burn away that devil of negativity forever! You are unique, different and really powerful but it's upto your determination, will-power and inner strength that will make you a winner or a sadist!

You can decide to be an optimistic person in this world of depressions and frustrations....

That's when You become a Winner of this Challenge and Step Forward with True Happiness in your life!... Every challenge can be won but you have to make your mind and your soul so strong that no devil in any form will even touch you! Please Stay Strong, Happy and Successful always with your trademark of Positive Energy.

#Happiness #successmindset

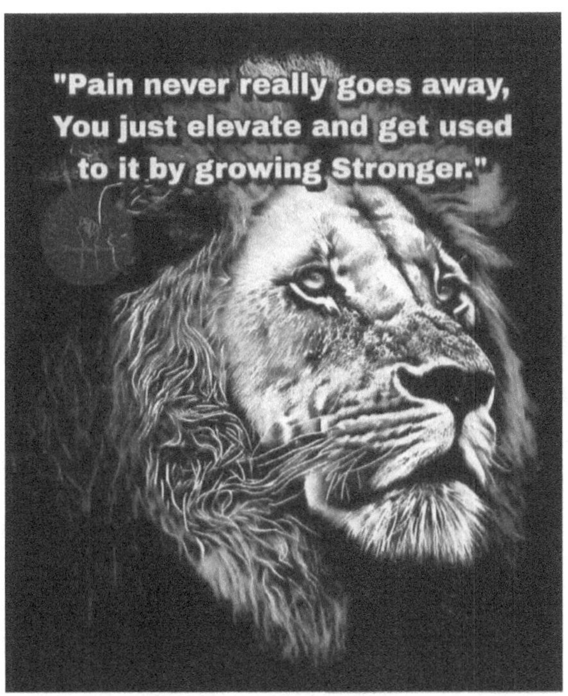

Can you move ahead without looking back in life?

I really feel that if you want to have positivity in life you should have tasted the negative situations which killed your morale...

First please look back at your wounds which stabbed your heart and soul. But after that you should also look how you overcome those crisis situations...Examine who was with you to console you the most and what actually made you overcome that challenge. You are the best judge of your mistakes and your victory. Please think and ponder over this state. You will feel good about how a situation which wounded you so badly has in the end made you a stronger person and made it a challenge won by you!

So my friend please stay strong and happy always. You are unique always.

#peaceofmind #stressmanagement #Happiness

Do you open your eyes and see everything with an open heart daily?

We all love to see what we want to see and accept only what suits our needs. When everything or maybe everyone behaves the way you want or expect them to behave, life is beautiful for many people. The moment anything changes or anyone behaves in the opposite manner, don't you feel hurt or get disturbed?

If your honest answer is yes then my friend you are a normal person and this is an absolutely normal reaction. To accept reality does burst many bubbles of dreams and believe me some hurt badly....these happen just to open your eyes to show you the naked truth of life.

Every individual is unique, different and has different capabilities. We have to accept them the way they are created by God or your Creator or else we will end up being critical Judges who are bitter and never happy or peaceful....

Letting go of your high expectations and accepting all humans as they are will make you happy and peaceful deep inside your soul. Once you are in peace deep within your soul only then can you can spread your peace to others in life!.....So please stay happy, content and blessed always .

#peacemaker #Happiness #mindfulness

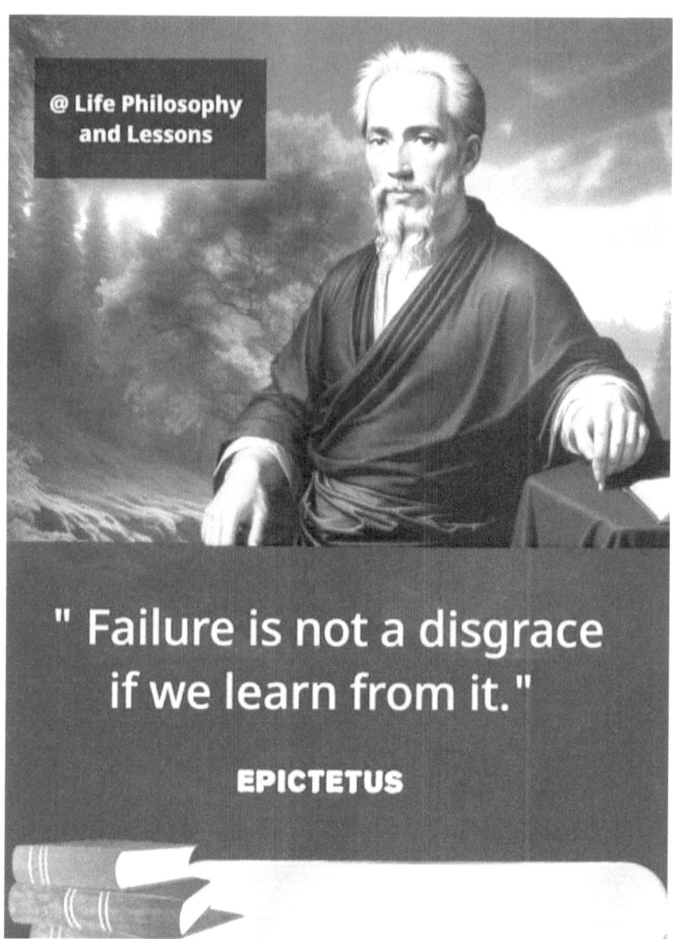

Is the fear of failure stopping you from stepping forward?

I truly understand this fear of failure which stops our hearts from moving forward in life. There are so many pressures which we are facing from so many areas (personal or professional) which build this fear deep inside us that we never take any risk ending up in never coming out of our comfort zone in life.

Many think that taking any risk is dangerous only as they fear they will have to face failure!

But if for once you take that golden step forward and step up strongly thinking that this time I have learnt my lessons because of my past failures....Then believe me my friend you have conquered this devil called fear already. Now your growth and confidence will increase and you will become successful surely! So please never fear my dear friend and throw those mini capsules of fear out of your sweet heart to drink the sweet potion of victory happily! You are unique and will feel invincible like a true champion or warrior in your life! Stay happy and blessed always

#successmindset #bravehearts

My silence means I am tired of fighting

and now there is nothing left to fight for. My silence means I am tired of explaining my feelings to you, but now I don't have the energy to explain them anymore . My silence means I have adapted to the changes in my life and I don't want to complain. My silence means I am on a self healing process and I am trying to forget everything I ever wanted from you. My silence means I am just trying to move on gracefully with all my dignity. –

Silence is silver or is it an undercurrent tremor?

I found these touching words which I shared in the picture today from an unknown source but it touched my heart piercing right through it...I was asked by my doctor to make my voice rest for 1 month at least. Yes to you it may be a small issue but for a person like me it was like God saying 'Shut up Surya!'...A chatterbox young lady whose voice is her identity from her music to speeches as a Toastmaster and always talking to family and friends. friends......Imagine how my extrovert nature which makes me truly myself with my affirmation to become very peaceful after reading them..

My quest ended when I got this magical answer to my questions. I found this small piece of prose while net surfing...

The magic transformed my feelings into happiness and pure peace...they said what my heart was deriving at finally.... Thanks for your patience to read and understand my state.... Please stay happy and blessed always.

#joyfulmoments #peacebuilding #mindsetforsuccess

Why do you fear failures in life?

We are living in a world where there are fears which are like the burdens of rocks on our minds stopping us from moving or even breathing freely sometimes. This could be fear of losing anything or anyone in your life depending on your most precious priority in life. This fear of hurting or losing your precious happiness actually restrains you from taking the best decisions in your life many times. Please prioritise your happiness and pursue that happiness with full passion and sincere dedication. You will excel and you will feel victorious in the end of this difficult and different process....

The satisfaction you will achieve will be enriching your mind, body and soul. That's why we all should be brave and beat our fears so strongly that one emerges as the true champion in life! Please rise and shine as you are unique and will be the best in your dream destination which leads to your happiness. Stay happy and blessed always.

#successmindset #determinationwins #Happiness

Do you love to be famous for your speed or your ethics?

This question is for everyone who is running for many reasons and still never satisfied or happy at any point in life. Yes I fully agree that speed in your actions help you in your works but slow pauses are important to think well and take care of your inner conscience too.

If you are becoming rich very fast at the expense of your fellow colleagues or sub ordinates' tears and hatred then no matter how much money you made as profits you will never get peace of mind in reality especially in the long run.

Similarly in your personal life its very easy to make a lot of friends but to retain the best ones as your best friends you will have to spend your time and love with patience for them which really requires lot of time in life.

Experiences will teach you a million lessons in your life which millions of money will fail to teach you only if you value wisdom more than money.

The same wisdom can never be stolen or grabbed from you but it only multiplies when you share it happily. Slow growth with good moral ethics is the real way and the best way to become truly happy and peaceful in your life.

So please relax, think about what are your real priorities in life and prudently walk towards success with a strong smile every day of your life. Organise your works with your team in such a way that all are happy to share their best always.

When your team is happy you will be double happy and together you will celebrate every success in your achievements. So please be happy, careful and hopeful always.

#happiness #successmindset #teambuilding #wisdom

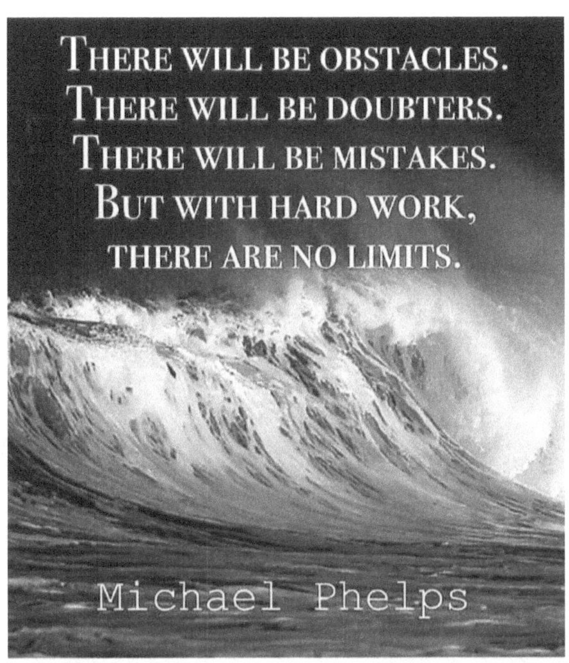

Are you chasing your dreams in your dreams or in reality?

Yes, we all have dreams and sometimes the sad failures we have faced in implementing these cherished dreams become our obstacles from trying again. The fear of failure and the pressure of losing many precious things often stops us from trying again in life.

But unless you swim and cross the stream you will never reach your goal or target in life! For that the first and biggest step is stepping or jumping into the water without even thinking of a drop of failure. Please have strong faith in yourself and in the power of your Creator, who has made you to rise and shine in life always! You can and you will break all barriers or jump across all hurdles only if you believe in the magic of the power both from your deep inner self and in the magical power of God or your Creator's divind hand for you!

So please move forward, pursue and work hard for fulfilling your dreams to become the super champion you can become in your life! Stay happy, brave and blessed always.

Even the most positive people have negative thoughts, the secret is not to feed them.

How do you face negativity?

Yes, I really would like to know especially in this world where we all are facing so many negative people and situations and ironically these same people say 'Stay positive' to you! I don't understand when many people preach huge lessons of positive energy and in their real lives they practice the opposite of these same virtues. There are lots of people ready with free advice on everything but I really get perplexed to take that advice from them when their actions are totally opposite from that advice!

So today I really get confused to trust people with their advice. On social media I have seen how fighting couples portray the most romantic poses in pictures! Some parents show off their children's achievements when they have actually never supported them in reality! Some people show fake grief on someone else's death to show off their status and friendship with that dead celebrity! All this is done and negativity is spread to such a great extent that you just cannot become positive for anything in life sometimes! All these fake positive advices is for selfish motives only and these are just an image building exercise. This is what I have realised after years of observation and experience....

Please stay true to yourself and show integrity in your words as well as actions. Please avoid pretensions and stop fake image boosters as that will make you really balanced in your emotions and expressions in your life! Negativity can be spread by others but please shield yourself from letting it affect you or your peace of mind. It's normal to cry, feel sad or mourn but please snap out of that sad state soon for your own best life and for all your loved ones who want to see you smile happily. Thanks for your sweet patience and understanding of my feelings today. Stay happy and blessed always.

#integrity #simplicity #peaceofmind #Trust #truthmatters

How long should you mourn over setbacks or failures in your life?

You are the best judge for your behaviour and the best critic for yourself but have you ever thought of becoming the best motivator for yourself?

Yes, my friend I really want you to become the best motivator for your own self! Please never forget that only if deep down in your heart you are strong then you will become double strong in your actions. You can and you will stand strong in front of any failures or setbacks! Please try to make this thought powerful inside you...that is...." I will defeat this devil called fear to achieve my goal, Come What May!"

Try not to waste too much time in wiping your tears and stepping forward in your life. The more you cry the more precious time you are losing and also you are making your loved ones cry for long too....

So wake up and smile to move ahead in your life and always remember that hope is stronger than fear. The bitter past can become a sweet future only if you take action today! Close the past door to stresses and open the new door to happiness with hope in your eyes and strength in your heart! Stay happy, hopeful and powerful always.

#happiness #dedicationtoexcellence #successmindset

Laughter is the best medicine so are you laughing enough to stay healthy?

Life has always been a mystery and we never know what we will face at what time...The more you laugh the more you can spread your positivity to yourself and all your fellow humans. Sometimes try laughing at your own self if you want to de-stress, by telling your situation and the reactions to your friends or family just like a story....Believe me even that helps you relax and eases your own stresses. You can try writing about it and then reading it aloud with a sweet laughter inside your room if there is no one to hear your story....

Just relax and breathe deeply and always remember you have survived your depression state like a strong warrior so you can laugh and be proud of yourself surely. Then this smile which is your most beautiful asset will shine bright and make you look like a Superstar always. Happiness radiates the best beauty in everyone. Please stay happy, joyful and blessed always.

#Happiness #peaceofmind #harmony

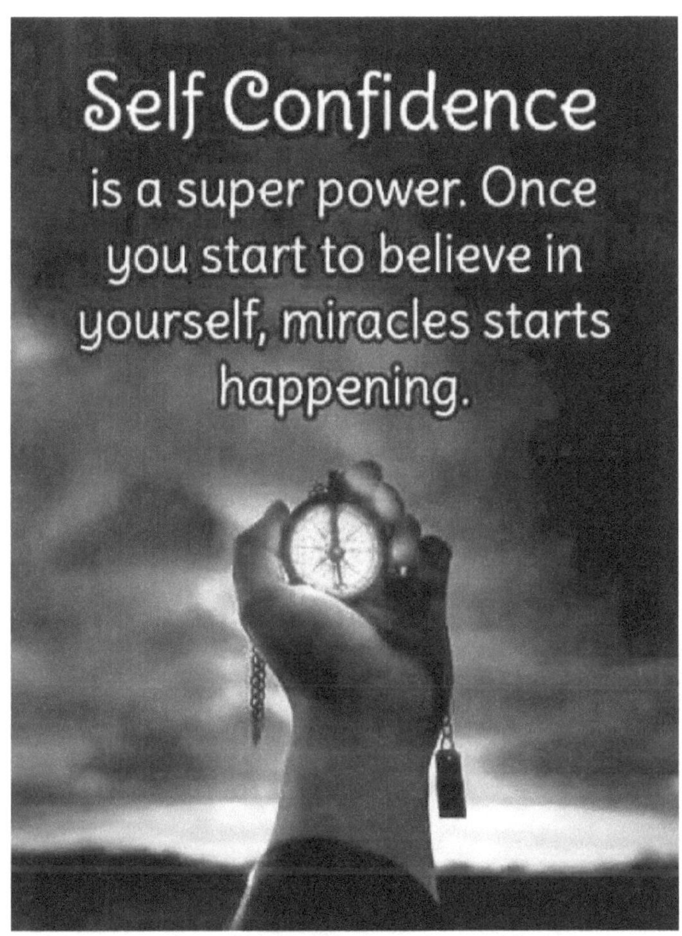

Do you believe in your inner strength to take you forward in life? Are the fears of failure, devilish mockers or different pressures blocking your steps to grow high up happily? Please wake up and throw away this shell of stubborn negativity before it's too late to rectify....

Yes it's the truth that life is unpredictable and many unexpected twists and turns await you at the most difficult times. If you don't start to step out of your fears or danger zones you will lose the most important thing in life...guess what...its the time you have left to live in this beautiful world!

Anyone who has a big terminal illness will understand how precious each moment of life is and it's that precious life you are wasting in tears, fears and regrets....Before you lose everything you have take a bold step and move ahead with full self-confidence to face life like a strong warrior who never quits!

You can and you will conquer your fears if you want and if you make your self-confidence the strongest super power inside you!

Please start strongly believing in yourself to make your self -confidence, your super power to excel in all your endeavors in life.Stay happy and blessed always.

#Confidence #Growth #successjourney

Be so busy
loving your life that
you have no time
for hate, regrets,
or fear.

Happiness is a journey or is it your final destination? This is something which can be debatable but have you ever wondered why? If being rich and famous is your goal or ambition then you can seriously pursue that...But why slog so badly and wait right till the old age of your life to enjoy those successful moments?

I really feel that after winning or even fighting every battle that your life throws on you, one really deserves a break to replenish your energy and relax your body and soul. How else will you gather more strength to fight better when the next challenge comes your way?

Life is a series of challenges like a relay race and the more to energise your mind and body the more powerful you become in future. So please seize your present time and make sure you are striking a good balance between work and play or pleasure. Remember all work and no play makes not only Jack a dull boy but you too!..Relish everyday like an ice cream before time melts away from your hands and leaves you with ugly sad and irreversible regrets...

Stay happy, hopeful and powerful always..You deserve that beautiful smile every day for sure.

#Smile #habitsforsuccess #Rejuvenation

The best revenge is to have enough self-worth not to seek it.

Are you seeking revenge without realising that this revenge is actually seeking to ruin you?

Just think for some time and make a list of your most precious possessions in life. Apart from the material things if you make a genuine list then most of you will have happiness, peace, good health and success in this list. Some of you may prioritise your ambitions while some may prioritise your family needs or your professional needs or just anything. But to be happy you must be so strong and focused with your goals that nothing becomes an obstacle in your path to success. If you keep comparing, complaining or keep grudges against your enemies then you will be ruining your peace, good health and your precious time of your invaluable lifetime.

So please focus on growing yourself in such a strong way that your worth increases many more times with a positive attitude. Just learn to forgive your enemies as they are just distractions and big rocks which never let you enjoy your own life's journey peacefully. By constructive use of your time you can ignore and let go of these blocks forever. Ultimately you will be winner and the most happy human being!

Your happiness will spread to your loved ones and spread more peace and harmony in your life. So please let go of those negative people and embrace your own positive self always. Stay happy, hopeful and powerful always.

#successjourney #peaceandprosperity #powerfuldecisions

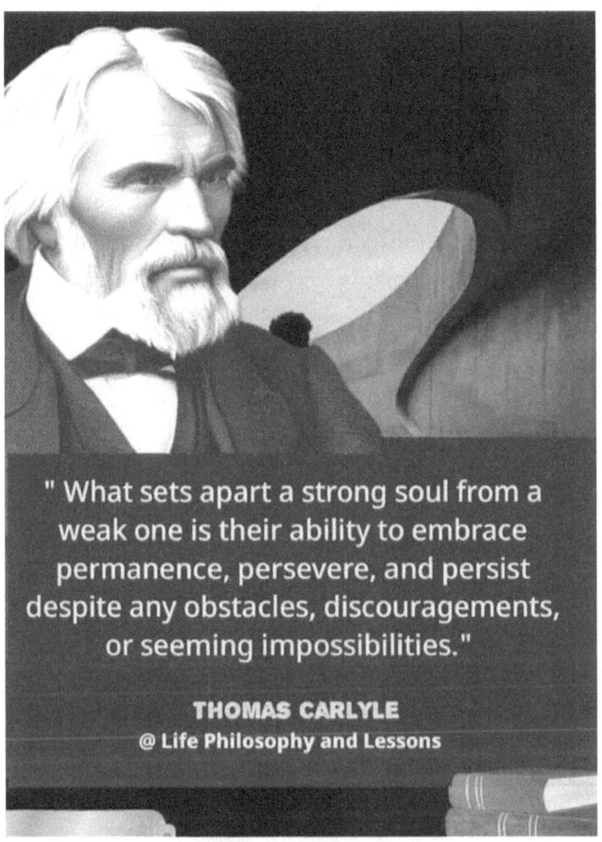

Are you a strong soul or weak soul?

You have the strength deep inside your heart and soul but have you ever wondered why this is not enough to fight the high level stress or challenges that life throws at you? I have seen how many people believe in many things which make them reliable on those very things like some people or lucky charms or even some irrational beliefs....

When you start to believing the good strong virtues of

your own character and sincerely work hard on becoming a stronger person with each challenge of life that's when you actually become a strong soul. The self-confidence and optimistic attitude will push you high up like the buoyant force and make you a real winner in life! Slowly and steadily your intelligence, your experience and your strong will-power will create in you the real champion who wins and strives to keep winning all the medals possible in his lifetime. So please throw away the weak factors which are the negative chains binding you and stopping you as obstacles from achieving what you deserve in life. Identify the problems and solve them before they grow beyond repair.

Wishing you a happy and successful life...Stay strong to rise and shine everyday like the Sun..

#strongmind #performanceimprovement#successmindset

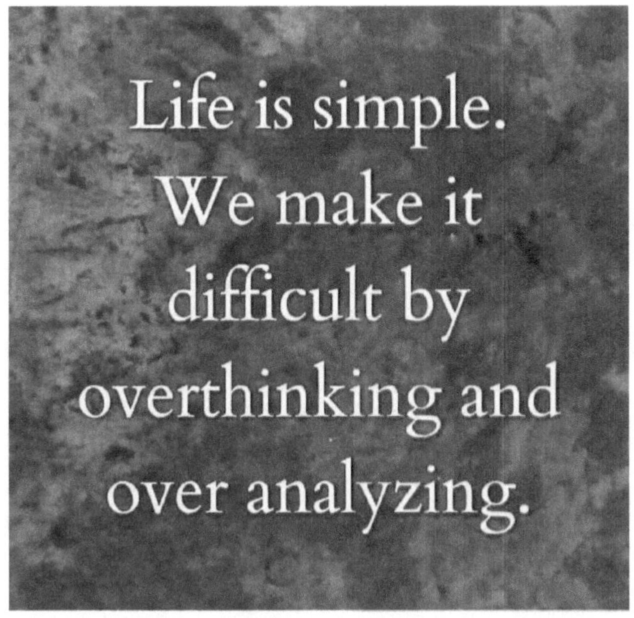

Are you rushing into too many things at the same time but finding it hard to be simply happy at any point of time?

Yes, life is getting very busy for many people and there is a race or competition which is making many people go crazy. The burnout in emotions is at unbelievably high levels in almost all age groups of humans today globally. This is a sad reality as most of the people are suffering from stress related issues which affects your health, personal and professional relationships affecting your life's peace and harmony in many ways...

Have you wondered why are we only hearing people complaining about their lives now? Why no one is truly happy deep inside their hearts? The reason shoots out many more questions but the only answer lies deep inside your own mind. Please take a deep breath and think if today you are a free bird flying in the sky and you have full freedom to do anything your heart wants to do! Will you be happy? Can you press the pause button on all your questions or thoughts for 5 simple minutes to think with a calm mind about all your favourite desires one by one. Make a list and you can fulfill your desires one by one but please don't rush in to fulfill all your wishes in one day.

Think about the simple pleasures of life which you can easily do and plan out how you are going to fulfill one dream one day. Keep it simple and realistic and you will be able to enjoy that happiness like a sweet ice cream....

Your simple smile, simple sweetness in your dreams all can be relished only if you relax and find some precious time for yourself and your loved ones. Everyone deserves a rest and happiness so you just enjoy that simply because you are always special and unique. No need of over thinking or over analysing matters which are not in your control. Try to forgive all your irritating enemies for some time. Simply speaking let all your worries flow away and fill that space with your favourite music or food or anything you love...

I am sure this simple life will make you happy and peaceful one day. So happy to see your patience to be with my thoughts till here. Wishing you a happy and peaceful life always.

#Life #peaceofmind #happiness

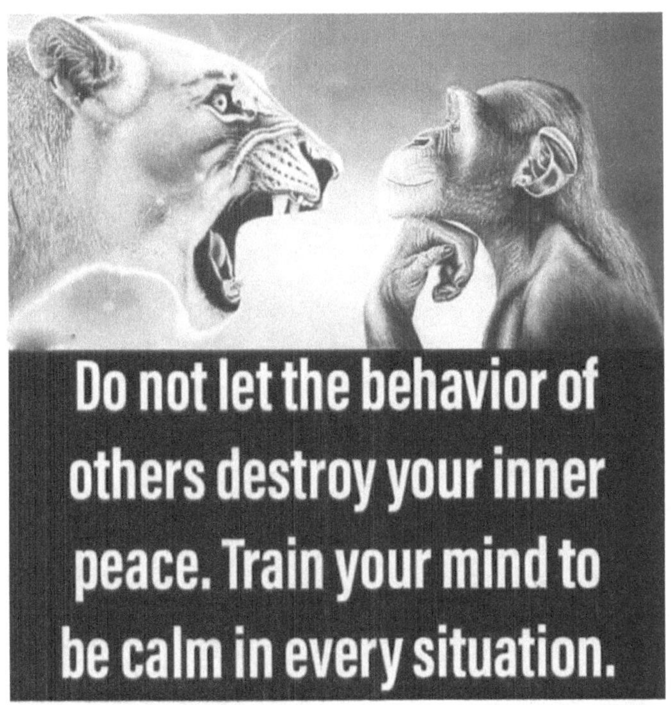

Are you a cool and confident person till someone irritates you beyond limits?

It's absolutely human to get irritated and disturbed by some people and many times anger takes over the angel inside you and hell breaks loose....

If you Master your own mind and train yourself to remain cool and calm during such adverse situations then believe me you are a true champion of life!

Yes, nothing can stop you from becoming super successful in life...

So what are you thinking now and why are you waiting to change? Please make yourself so strong, independent and powerful by making your mind stronger than your weak emotions....Surely you will become successful and happy soon....Make sure you stay happy always

#successmindset #determinationwins

Do you let your emotions overpower your behavior to make you angry or sad or do you make your emotions empower you to make yourself intelligent?

Yes...We all are humans and we all are emotional people with a soft heart which wants love, respect, happiness and understanding from others especially our loved ones. But have you ever felt bad when someone calls you an emotional fool especially when you take some important decisions in your life? They

say you are not practical and will repent later for this foolish-
ness....

As women and as mothers especially there are many situations in our lives where we sacrifice our happiness for others.
But do we get any reward or award or even a good word of gratitude from the very people for whom you sacrificed with so much
love and endured so many sufferings?...

That's the simple but painful question life asks you when
one day and your answer is left with regrets and tears only...

Please find your path to your happiness now and don't waste any
more precious time to convince or explain yourself to those un-
grateful people who don't value you or your loving heart. They
will realise their mistakes when you move forward in life boldly,
wiping your tears and step up with your golden confidence.

Please make your emotions your strength and never become a fool to please others! People are happy with you till you
serve them like a slave. They will appreciate and butter you with
sweetness only to get their work done from you. If you stay strong
emotionally then your intelligence will reward you surely. Use
your wisdom and maturity with prudence to live happily and
peacefully.

You can create your happiness so please pursue your
peace with a vengeance and your beautiful smile especially in
front of all your enemies. Believe me that's the best revenge and
you will be a true champion in life if you truly make your emotions your strength and not weakness! Thanks for your patience
to understand my thoughts...Please stay happy and blessed always

#hardworkpaysoff #emotionalintelligence
#determinationwins

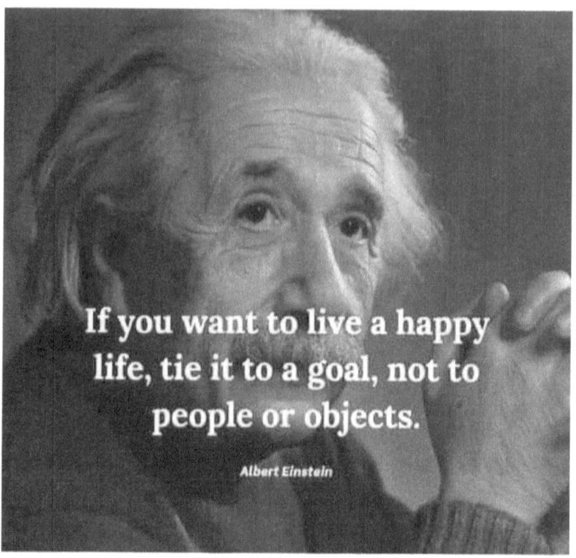

Are you a goal oriented person?

Life is full of unexpected challenges at unexpected times. If you are calm, strong and sensible then with maturity you will choose good goals to accomplish in your lifetime. But on the other hand if you depend on other people's satisfaction then you will keep trying on but in vain. Same thing happens when you find your happiness in riches, or possessions. Your thirst will increase and your quest will never end as the more one desires the more the number of desires increase with each accomplishment....

So what is the secret to true happiness or attaining a good satisfaction in life?

Please try to set realistic goals and be independent enough to realise them yourself. You and your hardwork to achieve your desirable goals should be in harmony with each other. In the end you will be satisfied and happy with your work. This will make you more confident to work more and get better with each attempt. Slowly but steadily you will become the master of your trade and the ultimate warrior who wins against all odds in life. So be happy, careful and blessed to achieve success in all your works in life always.

#successmindset #happinessmatters#intelligence

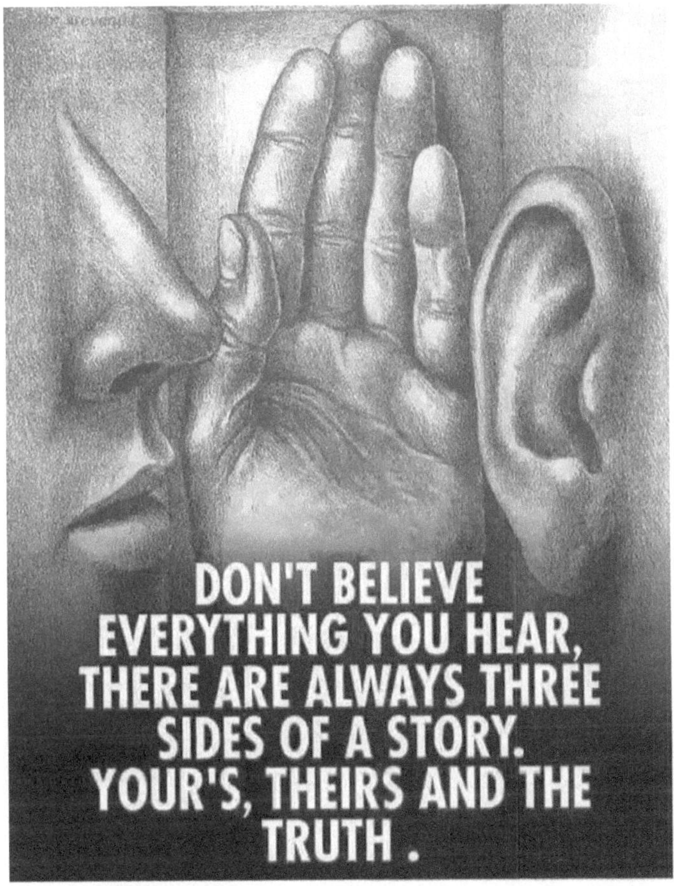

Are you too simple or are you too smart to be convinced easily by others?

Life is the biggest teacher and we all learn through our experiences every day....

So many people preach so many things that it is really very difficult to stick permanently to anyone person's thoughts or influences as they all fluctuate with time and circumstances.... Yes, there are different opinions of different people which shape our thoughts and affect our lives in so many ways.

But have you ever wondered why some people love gossiping and some people are too quiet to even give their own simple opinions to others? Many people are experts in manipulating your simple friendship to suit their own selfish motives without you even knowing! You just keep getting fooled if you keep trusting them blind folded...

To be strong and focused in your life both personally and professionally you must make your sense of judgement very fair and as rational as much as humanly possible.

Never fall for the sweet traps of sweet foxes like manipulating friends or anyone, who misuse your pure character traits to gain their selfish motives. You are your own guard and your mind should be so sensitive and intelligent that no one can sway you to their tunes, come what may!

So you can listen to others calmly but take your own decisions wisely especially with patience, to be successful and truly peacefully happy in your life. Hope that you are happy, peaceful and blessed in your life always.

#simplejoys #successjourney

Do you believe than distance makes the heart go fonder?

Have the past few Covid years of physical distance ever affected your personal relationships or your professional relationships so seriously that you wanted to run away from this whole world? You then wished to sit alone in a beautiful beach or on the top of a wonderful Mountain peak? Away from all the non-stop yelling mobile phones, glaring computer screens , never ending pressures of some humans demanding some work or the other at gun point or unrealistic, unreasonable deadlines....

My friend if you have been even once in this situation I can perfectly understand you. I understand that you are working very hard to make everything work as well as possible without hurting anyone else in this tough grinding situation. What you really need now is pure rest, peaceful atmosphere and happiness of being you and enjoying your existence as a good hearted human being full of love and laughter! Some people may say you need a break or small vacation to relax, restore and replenish your body,mind and soul...all different advices will flow like waterfalls around you...But please choose your own fountain of happiness and stay there happily alone for some precious days or even hours at least! Understand what you love to do in life and pursue your love with peace of mind...I promise you will come out happily after these few moments of solitude and peaceful pleasures of life. You will know that all your personal and professional relationships can wait for some moments only if you allow them to wait for you! Everyone is enjoying their life and you too deserve to enjoy your life. You are unique and stay unique, different as well as happy by loving yourself first and taking good care of yourself in every possible way! All successful relationships need some freedom and space to flourish and grow stronger especially with time. Every seed only becomes a tree when it is given the freedom to germinate, and spring with life as a beautiful tree one day. Enjoy you life's journey with yourself first and then bring in all your loved ones to join you with happiness and peace. Keep all your relationships strong as the roots and no distance will ever break these strong relationships of your life. Trust me you are and you will be happy and positive only if you daily strive to be like that especially when life is throwing challenges to your face every day....Please be careful, happy and strong in your heart and soul always. Take care and best wishes to you to flourish forever and ever..

#Happiness #peaceofmind #successmindset

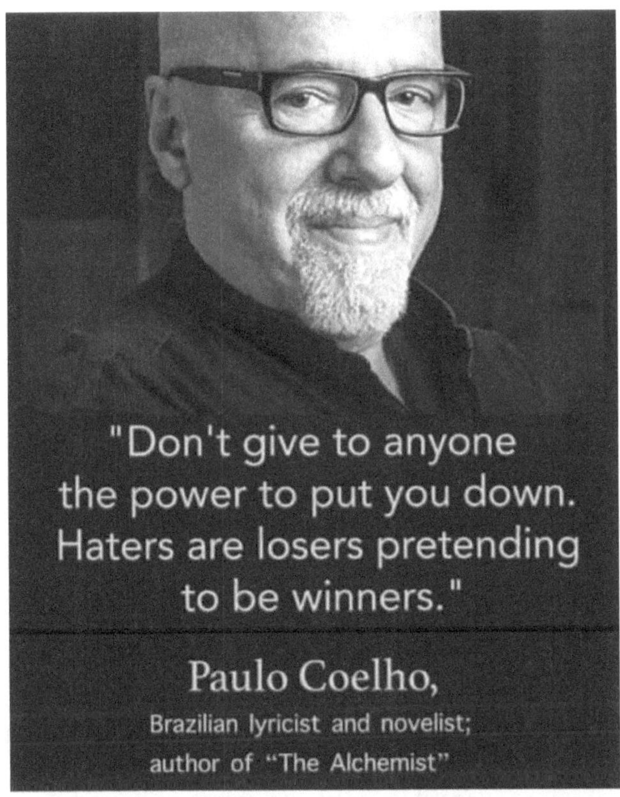

Do you have an experience of your best friend or your trusted partner stabbing you behind your back to gain his or her personal motive? I mean that did anyone you trusted and loved like your own soul ever hurt you and you understood this betrayal too late to even react normally?

Today let me confess that I have had many real life experiences where sometimes in both my professional and personal life where people misused my goodness in values and then later got away after denying me my rightful things like some important posts, prizes, money etc....Till now they have not even apologised to me! I have felt horrible at those weak moments and it really took me some time to overcome from those emotionally sad days of my life!...But the one thing which kept me going was the strong moral values and principles which are deeply embedded in my soul. Thanks to my God, my close family members and true best friends, who stood strongly with me in all my life's battles.They made sure that I never break myself down beyond repair!...Today I gather my courage to share with you this post just because of this strength which was built-up over many years.

I am highly grateful for all the strong support system that almighty God has given me which never lets me say I quit forever from life. I trust the power which whispers deep within my heart saying that 'Surya you cannot die in darkness..you have to Rise and shine'... 'God has made you to rise and shine that's why He named you Surya or Sun in English....'You are my (God's) favourite daughter and you will never fall forever....till you reach me up in heaven when I call you.'

This divine voice makes me rise from ashes like a phoenix and yes I rise and shine with a bright smile...

Please never let any haters or horrible people let you fall down and make you so depressed that you end your life's journey in any disastrous ways! We all are special and unique as we are the most special in God's creations...'Humans'..

There are no two humans with the same finger print so how can there be a duplicate of you? You are precious to your Creator God and to your family as well as your best friends.

No replacement is possible for you so please smile and stay strong in adversities as this is just a phase which will pass definitely. As Charlie Chaplin once said so rightly, "Nothing is permanent in this world not even our troubles".

All the sad phases in your life will pass away and your sun of hope and happiness will rise again surely. Be patient and strong in your faith and please be double strong in these weak moments. To conclude my humble request to you is that please never give anyone whatsoever or whomsoever the power to ever put you down!..Make sure you are very powerful deep inside your heart and soul to be truly a winner or champion in life! Please rise and shine in your life always

Do you love yourself? Do you want to show the world how great you are?....Are you like the Superstar or Super Powerful Sun?

If you really want to shine like the powerful Sun or King of the Solar System then please make yourself that golden drop of sunshine which when it falls on others actually illuminates them as heroes!......Make your sweet Ray of Sunshine so beautiful that to see themselves as powerful Superstars they will need your Ray of Sunshine, hope, and peace!....Yes my friend if you show others the best path of life, then you will become that lamp of light which is illuminating the world we are living in at present...So to become powerful you must have a basic team of strong rays which makes you look and feel like the Sun or King of the Solar system!...I hope you understand my humble request so that you inspire others first and let them glorify your actions in real life! So please shine bright and make your life path full of hope, peace and harmony for all others who see your light which shines bright from deep within your soul...Please stay happy, hopeful, and smile beautifully every day...You are unique and stay strong always...

Are you a fighter who is highly aggressive and assertive in all your opinions with every one you meet in life?

If your answer is yes, let me ask you that are you truly happy especially in your relationships both personally and professionally? I have a feeling that you might be feeling happy but others are unhappy with you....I mean they are expecting some apologies or simple courtesy from you which you are not giving it to them as per their desires.....

Many problems in life come when one thinks that he is right always and forces others to behave the way he wants them to behave everywhere.There will be difference of opinions with many people everywhere. You can ignore others but at some point in your life you will yearn for good friends and good relationships which are very important, to stick with you but they will leave you as soon as they find an excuse...

Do you win this fight or do you become the sad warrior who is alone all life. If you are ready to take this advice then my friend please try to lose an argument with your best friend or your superior or boss or your wife or parents and make then feel like a great winner! This loss is actually a sign of victory and not failure...

You are special and unique just like the Sun. Yes if you are an intelligent person you will know where or when to fight and when not to fight! Your silence and smile is enough to silence your critics or enemies sometimes! Let them think they won and you show that you are learning from them in life! Slowly your hardwork, dedication and perseverance will lead you to great success in life!

#success #learning #people

Have you heard the song, 'Fools rush in where angels fear to tread but I can't help falling in love with you' ???

Yes my dear friends, if you hurry you will worry but if you patiently walk or softy jog you will enjoy your journey always...So please enjoy life with its ups and downs so that when you are tired and you look back you can tell your children that I did all this in my life and at every step I enjoyed my challenges before winning them or losing them!

Life is not a mad race but a joyride but it all depends on the person who is taking that special ride either on foot or on a bicycle or in a car....You decide and you perform all your feats to become the true warrior or champion from the beginning to the end....Believe me you will fall in love with yourself and all your blessings be it in family, friends or your riches....You will be the best and feel the best always!

Please stay happy and blessed forever and never lose hope till your last breath.

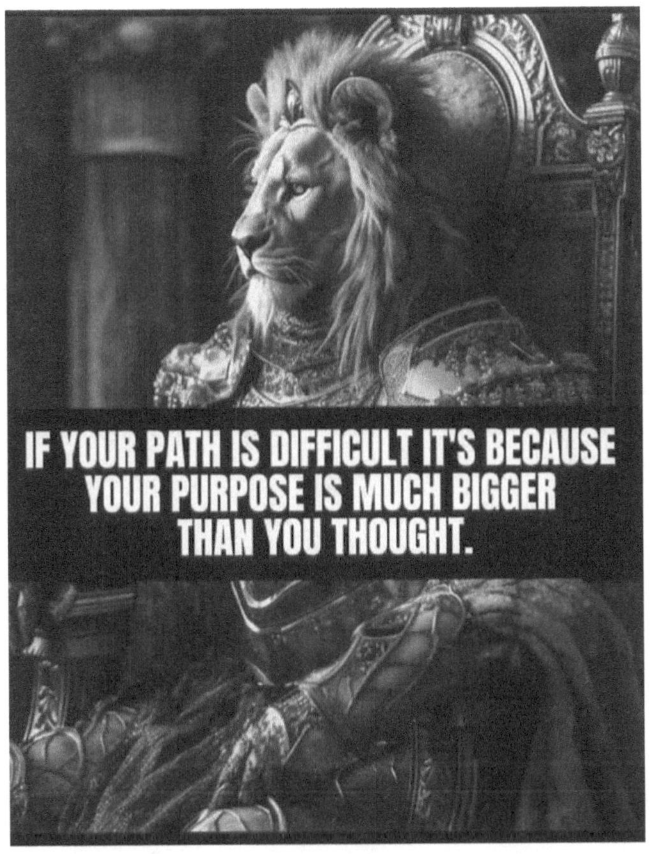

Do you give up easily in life when you face challenges that life throws unexpectedly right on to your innocent face mercilessly?

Please sit back and think about the last setback you faced in your life which made you say 'I Quit'...now never again!

Please try pressing the Rewind button into a past experience will make you understand what I am trying to say now. Now please pause there and put your present self with a second chance to change your reaction to that failure situation!

Can you feel that now with time you have emerged stronger and have become a slightly wiser version of yourself!

Yes...You are born for a higher calling in life and your purpose in life is the pursuit of a higher goal...That's why you were being prepared by that small failure to receive greater rewards in your future! So for bigger success you need to give bigger sacrifice, dedication and perseverance both at a double power to pep you up...really high up!

So never forget this and dare you if you ever give up in life my friend who has so much patience for endurance!

You have the power deep inside your soul and please find it first and you are the champion you are destined to be in your life! Please rise and shine like the beautiful Sun or Surya(Sanskrit name for our Sun)...You are special and unique always...So please stay happy and blessed always...God bless you.

#success #experience #future #power #change #like

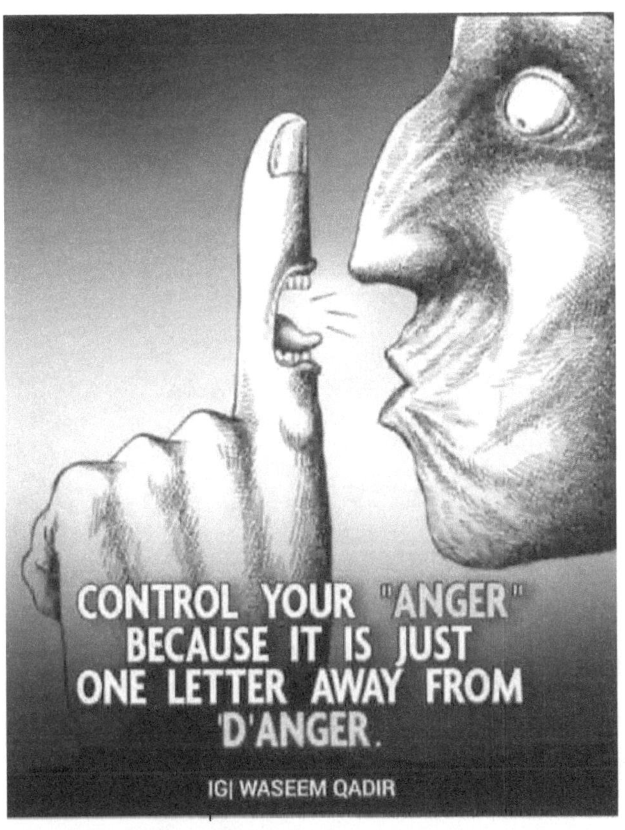

Do you love yourself and your family?

Please stop burning yourself with anger as seriously it harms you more than the person or situation which has forced you to become angry! When you raise your voice on someone you are creating the worst image for yourself in front of your opposition. More than this ego or pseudo image you are killing your own respect too. Any relationship to sustain needs validation at different stages especially with love and respect. So you decide if 5 minutes of anger is more precious than your own family.

#love #respect #relationshipbuilding #teambuilding

Do you see your calmness as a Superpower?

Please give your valuable views on this question. Thanking you in advance for your patience and time. Stay happy and blessed always.

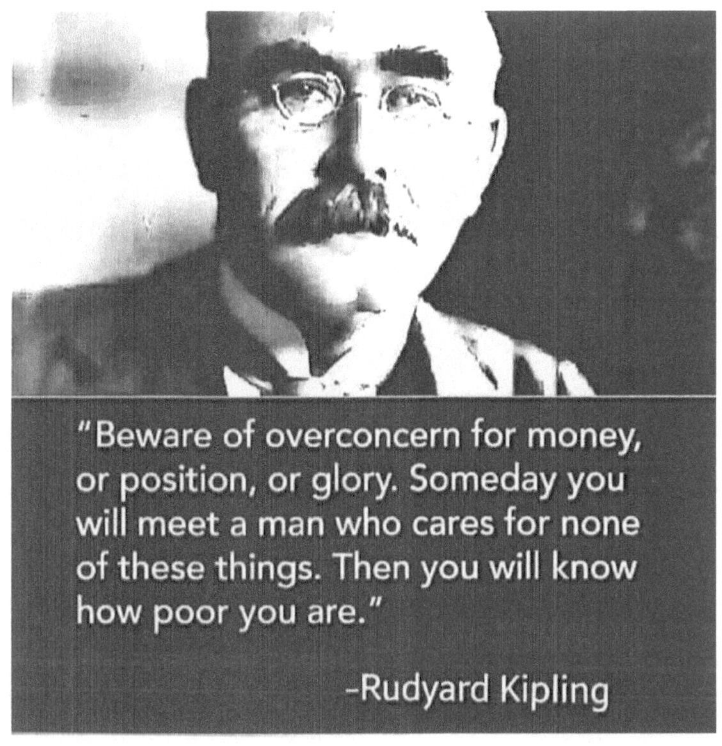

Are you an intense and highly passionate kind of person who wants to excel in everything in life at the earliest?

If your answer is yes, then my friend please calm down and press the pause button on your brain for 5 mintues for me...Please understand that excess of anything or desire or even emotions can become harmful to you in the long run. Please be alert and mindful of so many vices or negative influences that ruin your most precious possession in life...Yes your own 'Peace of Mind' and the peace of your family and colleagues......

Please 'Guard' your inner circle of family and friends but

more than that please 'Guard' yourself from negative thoughts, negative people to stay peaceful for your full life....

Money is a necessity but not everything in life. People who are now falling on your feet can be for many reasons but you have to judge as to what gains he is getting on doing this? Friendships are being misused and families are drifting apart in this race for making money, fame and lack of communication is creating so much stress and hatred in this world.

Let us try sincerely to build the bridges of hope, peace , blessings and unity in integrity with all our fellow humans. Let us make this present world a better world for us, our children and our older generations...

Stay happy and blessed always .

Peace # Unity# Intergrity #happiness #successmindset

How you see yourself and work hard on improving your own self will determine how successful and happy you become in your life! So please stay receptive, humble and be a learner in all your ages and stages in life. You will be the best version of yourself each time you over come the challenge life throws on you unexpectedly. Stay happy and blessed always.

#hardworkpaysoff # Determination #success

What's more important to you, Money or Friendships?

Many humans world over are facing many challenges today especially with the need and sometimes greed for more money to maintain themself and their families. There are many people for whom any amount of money is never enough, so they keep running all the time towards ways and means to make money by hook or crook.

I have the personal experience of how people first create

a friendship with you and then after you donate money for them out of love, they betray you after their need is over. They play a victim card and start by sharing their sob stories, then praise you for your goodness till you are forced to help them. That is the modus Operandi of many frauds. So beware of friends who are only after you for cheating you by taking your money first and then even if they have it they will never return even a small portion of it back to you when you need it.

Yes, money does create enemies especially when you refuse to share it with others. But if you use your wisdom and maturity then you can save your emotions and your money from draining away. No one can steal your wisdom so please focus on building your wisdom both practically and emotionally. That's the best way to be happy and peaceful in life. You can always limit your sharing amounts and balance your own losses accordingly. Give only as much as that amount doesn't make you or your family a pauper. Be alert of fake friends and cruel friendships....

Just guard your peace and wisdom so that you are happy always in life. Thanks for your patience to read and spend your precious time for understanding my humble views. Stay happy and blessed always .

#share #experience #help #building #love #people #money

Can you face any fear in your life fearlessly?

Fortune favours the brave and yes my dear friend if you are brave enough to face the challenges that life throws at you then you are and you will be the champion in life! You are powerful enough to beat any devil only if you make the angel inside you strong enough!

So please make the Lion of Light and Wisdom grow Strong within You and with your Confidence and Strong Willpower you will be the Leader always. Please Cheer Up and stay strong come what may in life. Stay happy and blessed always.

#leader #mindsetmatters #determination #successmindset

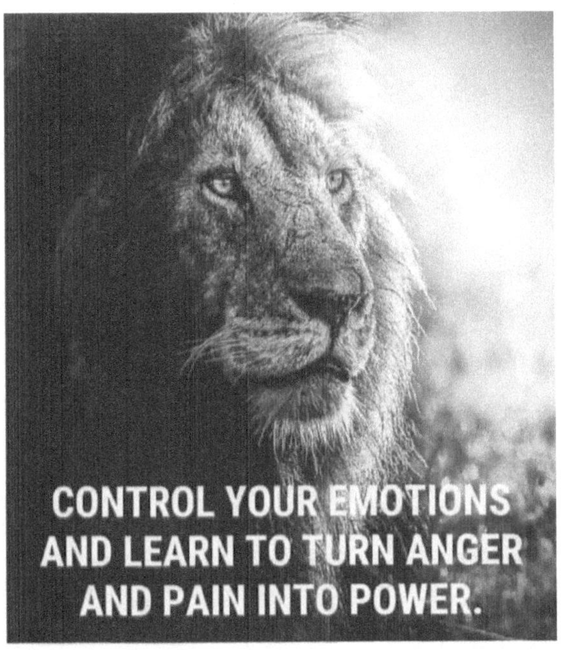

Are you powerful enough to face the real world?

The Youth of the world faces many challenges and no matter what the old generation preaches things are very different and difficult for our modern younger generations. Almost everyone is facing anger issues, stress management issues, Time Management issues , personal health issues and many psychological issues in these critical times of our present world. That's the sad reality and if you can face this giant devil with a cool and calm mind the. you have won your battle half way already.

So control your anger and channelize that energy into more constructive thoughts and use that energy to make yourself motivated enough to become a true winner or champion in your life! With confidence and great wisdom you will step ahead in life and reach the pinnacle of the glory you truly deserve in your life one day. So please make yourself internally so powerful that you control yourself in every situation to make it favourable for you. Thanks fir your patience and hope you stay patient always. Stay happy and blessed always.

Do you appreciate your own self or do you just keep feeling low about yourself in comparison to others?

Comparison kills the joy of your life and people who always keep comparing themselves with others are never truly happy and peaceful in life. Many people keep complaining about how some others are more successful or are lucky and they wish they were born as lucky as them.

But when ever you do so you are actually creating a negative energy inside yourself and verbally too spreading that negativity to others in your life. For instance you keep telling your employees or your children or even your spouse that what they have is not good enough. Surely the morale of those people will go down. They will feel bad about themselves. They will react with negativity too and no one will be happy in reality.

If on the other hand you appreciate yourself each time you accomplish any task very well and pat your own back with a smile. Then you will appreciate others for the works they are doing in life too. Once

you are positive you will definitely spread that positivity to others too. This on going process of gratitude and appreciation will always help you build great relationships both profession-ally and personally. Please try to be cheerful, honest and kind as that's what will make you peaceful and happy always. Fall in love with yourself and stay in love with your personality so that you grow beautiful and happier every day. Yes you will enjoy every moment of your life's journey in this beautiful way. So please stay happy and in love with yourself to be truly successful and rich in peace and spread harmony in your life. May Good Hope, a Sweet Smile and wise sweet words full of appreciation be en-riched in you today and always. Stay happy always.

#success #peoplemanagement

#energy #gratitude #react #help

Do you love your dreams?

If your answer is yes then please work hard to make them true! If your answer is no then please keep sleeping forever and never complain about others who are successful in their lives! If you want to be a winner in life then you should wake up first and then follow your dreams with great passion and dedication. Winners are not made in dreams alone...they work hard in reality to become Winners in real life. Thank you for your patience and understanding. Stay happy and blessed always .

#work #thankyou #love #mindsetmatters #success

Do you have full control on yourself especially when you are facing turbulent times?

Self control is the biggest control and yes its like the best remote control to your own mind which makes you a Master or King of all trades or the talents you possess in yourself! So please try this magic potion and slowly you will Master all your fears to live life like a true triumphant warrior .

#mindsetmatters #hardworkpaysoffs #success

Do you flaunt your knowledge to everyone all the time?

There are some people who love to preach and they hardly practice what they actually preach. They have a feeling that by showing off their knowledge they make themselves powerful enough to actually make others feel bad.

Yes my dear friends, if you keep preaching you are not actually doing any good unless you show your richness in your good character conduct.

It's your good behaviour which will last in others hearts and influence their minds in reality. So along with your rich knowledge please show your richness in your good moral values in your character by expressing that in your behaviour with your fellow humans.

A golden heart with a wise mind and matching actions, is the ideal combination for the most successful humans in this world. They rule your hearts and they are the true leaders. So please grow strong in wisdom and good character together to be the shining jewels on this beautiful earth. Stay happy and blessed always.

Are you ready for facing challenges that life loves to throw on you?

Yes my dear friends , if you really want to grow and change into a confident leader and successful human being both personally and professionally then you should be always ready to take all the different challenges life keeps throwing on us.

There are health problems, financial problems, family problems ,Office peer pressure problems and personal problems, and the list of problems are endless...But if you decide that you will face each problem like a challenge and fight it like a strong warrior then I assure you that you are the winner for sure!

This change that is seeing a problem by facing it first and then boldly overcoming it using your intelligence and will- power will make you confident, and you will change for your better each time. Yes, you will change and become that true warrior who commands respect and true love from all good hearted noble human beings...So stay strong and be a winner always..Thank you for your understanding and patience for reading my words till here. Stay happy and blessed always.

#health #thankyou #change #power #leader

#respect #intelligence #love #like

Do you change your attitude to people whenever there is a change in their positions?

Respect and sweetness in inter- personal behaviour specially changes in people's behaviour whenever there is a change in someone's position in life. Some people continue respecting and behave in the same way while we see a majority of people changing thier colours like a chameleon to suit their own conveniences.

Life teaches us lessons as experiences. If your behaviour is sweet, courtesious and empathetic right from the beginning in any relationship then you are truly a successful human being. If you stop behaving with good manners as soon as someone loses his position then you have to be very careful as you can expect a backlash or revenge from the same person one day when he comes back to that position. Some people become so rude that you feel very bad for them and this broods unnecessary negativity to ruin everyone's peace and harmony.

Ranks and titles are all temporary and they change from time to time. What should never change is your good behaviour and good moral conduct as that's your greatest treasure. This special treasure filled with good moral values will bring you respect, love and happiness always. Be strong, beautiful and polite everyday with everyone irrespective of their ranks. Fairness in your attitude, integrity and being respectful in your actions and words will make you a winner of hearts and truly a very happy human. This is the best legacy you can leave in this world to be remembered with love by everyone. Please stay happy and spread your beauty as your good moral values especially in your character always. Thanks for your patience and understanding to read till here.

#peoplemanagement #love
#change #happiness #beauty #respect

Are you calm in your natural reactions in your life's battles or do you fight like a warrior till your enemy is defeated?

I know our reaction buttons in our brain is triggered very fast and in these stressful times our normal reactions to negative situations is full of anger, bad words and hatred for the opponent....sometimes the revenge is never over. Have you ever thought why? The real reason is hidden deep in your mind and heart. You are not happy with yourself and these internal conflicts of your thoughts and other pressures which could be from your family or friends or loved ones or professional pressures, are actually making you bitter day by day. This is like a layer of dirt covering your true goodness of your heart. Your intentions are not wrong or dirty but your reactions are hurting others in many ways...

Please find out the real reason for your behaviour with patience and retrospective attitude by rewinding these precarious situations and inter changing the characters in it....

Simply think that if you are your enemy then how would you react in that situation. Slowly you will realise your mistakes and this realisation will make you happy. You can and you will try to amend these mistakes and start afresh in your relationships. Slowly and steadily you will become calm and be happy with yourself. Yes my friend you will fall in love with yourself! This will make you calm and you will be the ultimate winner in all your life's battles.

Many famous quotations by many successful personalities can be displayed by me to impress you and prove my thought's validity. But nothing is more precious than your own experience. I strongly believe its YOU who decides what's best for you and the best way to learn is by thinking for yourself with honesty. So relax and think with a calm mind to win in all your life's battles and please love yourself everyday....Stay happy and blessed always.

#experience #love #react #mindsetmatters #peaceofmind #relationshipsmatter #Happiness

Are you tired of working hard and ready to give up after years of struggle?

If yes then please never give up hope as your hardwork and perseverance is being put to test just like every metal is heated before becoming its best form. You will see the rewards soon and all you have to do is to believe in yourself especially the powers that the almighty God or your creator has filled deeply inside you.

I hope you shine bright like a diamond which also became diamond after years of suffering only...The spark in you will make you shine bright and you will get your dreams fulfilled one day. Stay happy and blessed always.

#like #Hope #Hardwork #Dedication #Happiness

Do you only dream or do you work to make your dreams true?

Planning and working hard to make your dreams a successful reality is very important in life. If you only dream then its a big waste of your emotional happiness....so when you wake up please try to make these dreams a reality and a happy reality one day! Stay happy and blessed always, take care my friends.

#work #happiness #planning # #success

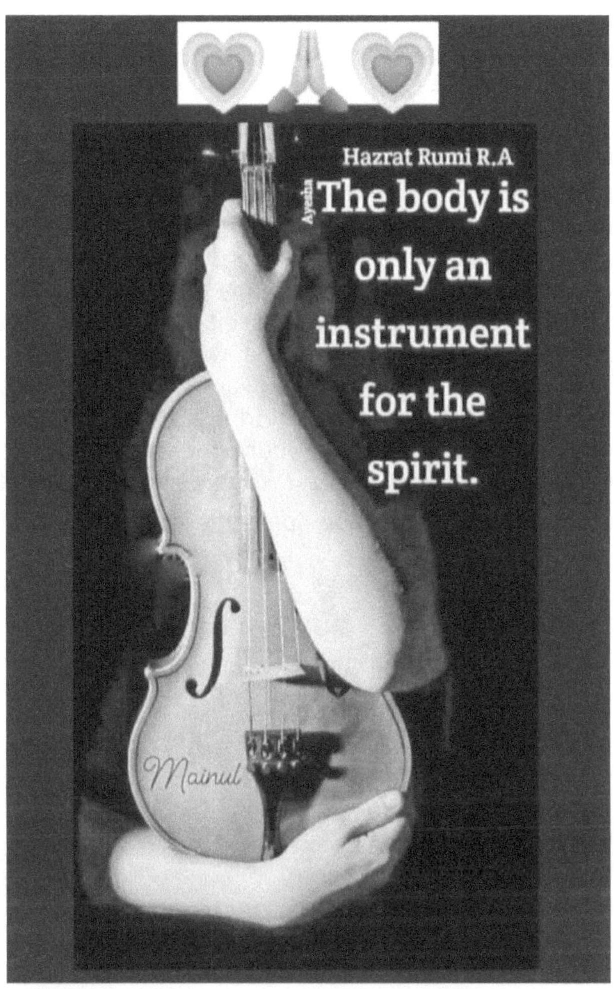

Are you thirsty for grabbing everything and being rich beyond any limit?

Yes it is true that many of us want money, riches and fame beyond limits! But have you ever wondered why? or have you ever pondered what you will do after you get all these in your real life? I have made a list of things to do and buy once I win my Million dollar lottery one day...Believe me this list is so funny sometimes that my family laughs uncontrollably at my humour and my husband ends up telling me that please make this your topic of speech in your next Humourous Speech contest! Yes my friend I am a Journalist and a Toastmaster so gift of the gab comes handy with the gift of my words....

One day seriously I pondered and thought that if I don't enjoy my present happiness and only keep planning for my future parties then I am actually ruining this present time! How much can you spend on luxuries and till what point do you do this? If you are alive only till then my dear friend ...So please value your present happiness in yourself, your family,friends and achievements, to be happy with the sweet necter of gratitude and abundance in peace....I hope you are selective and wise with your choices in life and now never drink from anything or everything offered to you! Thanks for your patience to understand my humble thoughts till now. Please take care and be happy always .

#future #money #gratitude #planning #happiness #dollar

Do you believe in this power of spirit?

The Spirit to beat any block or hindrance to emerge as a winner is what makes the human spirit the strongest power. When we overcome the challenges that life loves to throw at us, we become stronger with a strong spirit to overcome! The choice is to actually grow in your spirit and become more powerful than any adversity..So stand strong in your spirit and emerge as a champion in reality..Please stay happy and successful in life.

#power #happinessmatters

Are you strong enough to control your reactions?

Yes, if you can control your mind's reaction button then you are a winner in life's battles already! Make your smile your reaction to who all want to see your tears or your sad face. I promise you that's the best way to show your revenge in your sad times.

Your silent smile and your true inner strength will kill your enemies in the most peaceful way! So why not take up this blessed weapon and work hard towards your success in life. I assure you that this one step with confidence will definitely lead you to success and the lion within you will laugh with a bigger growl surely!

You can and you will win as its all about controlling your mind with this magical reaction button which is actually in your own hands!

So my friend please never feel bad and helpless in your failures as really your failures are the best lessons of life which will make you the most successful human one day! Please smile and quietly work hard with the Lion within you alive...and you will shout out with a beautiful victorious growl one day! Please stay happy and blessed always

#work #success #determination #peaceofmind

#Perseverance #Happiness

Are you so angry that you want to crush your enemy now?

Think after taking 3 deep breaths...Really if you get so angry that you want to thrash someone for not understanding you or hurting you then please for your own good health's sake take 3 deep breaths...and in each breath tell yourself you are powerful and you will never let this situation overtake your power....

Please you tell yourself that I will calm down and the relax myself first and only then think if I should react here...in the 3rd last deep breath you will calm down automatically and the magic of peace will start in your heart!

The revenge is for fools and anger harms you much more than your opponent! If you can control your anger and the reaction at that spur of a moment you have won this battle already...Slowly after you calm down then you can think how to counter this negative situation and then you will see how good ideas come into your calm mind. So you have now conquered your anger and won this battle against your opponent in the best way for yourself! If you got it then you are smart and powerful in your mind always...you are successful and will win many rewards in your life's journey. Thanks for your patience and please stay happy by being calm always. Stay happy to spread your happiness too.

Are you afraid to do something and feel like you are not fit for it?

Yes, there is a hidden fear which most of us have, which grows deep within our hearts and makes you doubt yourself!

It's very unfortunate that many are not wise enough to follow these tantras...or tricks of these things which hold back their steps.. You live only once and you cannot bring back time so please don't try to do that too!

Move forward happily and stay confident in all that you do in life. Remember that to fly high even an archer pulls back the bow but that doesn't stop the arrow from flying high and hitting the target with the bang on sound! So cheer up and push yourself upwards with confidence always. You are and will always be a winner in life!Thanks for your patience for understanding my thoughts.I hope you excel and never repel to be happy always.

#like #Happiness #Confidence #successmindset

Do you appreciate those people who never give up on you? Many people preach a lot of things when you seek them in your difficult times but when it comes to genuine help in action they all leave you alone. But there are some really special people who support you both in action and words..Have you ever wondered why or what they get in return?

Yes I am referring to your good friends, family and well-wishers who genuinely support you in your difficult times. All they expect back from you is gratitude and appreciation for their sincere efforts. If you show gratitude and respect to them then your life will be always full of love, happiness and peace. So what are you waiting for...make a list of your dear ones and spread your loving gratitude towards them as soon as possible. Life is too short for regrets and misery....

Just let go of complaints and see the brighter picture to make yourself happier.

Please try to appreciate your precious circle of angels in disguise and embrace your own happiness in multiple ways to live a beautiful life always. I hope you stay happy and blessed always .

Let us bring true joy in our lives by enriching our thoughts. For this purpose I am sharing these famous words by Rabindranth Tagore

(1861-1941)

R.Tagore explaining a verse of the Upanishads,

in his book "Sadhana-The Realisation of Life"-

Upanishads say "From joy does spring all this

creation, by joy it is maintained, towards joy

does it progress, and in to joy does it enter."

Tagore explains...

It means that God's creation has not its source

in any necessity;it comes from his fullness of

joy; it is his love that creates, therefore in

creation is his own revealment."

Another famous song in Rabindra sangeet says, "Anandu Loke Mangala Loke...Birajo Satya mangalam..." (Joyful world is an auspicious world! Hail the truth which is truly a Joy!)

Please stay joyful and spread your peaceful joy to your loved ones and all who truly matter to you in life!

Sharing a very important and great virtue of our life with you today. The great precious blessings of all our elders in family, teachers and care givers circle is the priceless reward we earn for giving them this honour. We also show our younger generation this great value through our genuine actions. Later we get that honour from them when they practice this value! Although this moral value is taught in all religions and many ancient cultures globally its practice is getting rarer with time today. The number of Old age homes or shelters for the aged senior citizens of the world is increasing rapidly. Especially as they need costly medicines and good medical care in old age which is the biggest common excuse most adults say before dumping them there! They hardly realise how cruel and thankless they are in reality! Let's all wake up before it's too late and do our duties for honouring them and showing our children this by our own actions rather than just preaching. I hope this is understood in full empathy and sympathy by all our wonderfully wise readers. Please stay happy and blessed everyone!

Please try to burn away your stress and worries with a good laugh and sweet sleep.

Anything that worries you will not last forever. You will live to see a better day if you just keep trying without expecting too much. If you live peacefully and spread your peace to all who meet you in life, then you are the true leader in life. A leader who rules the hearts of his loved ones and your treasure will be full of love, happiness, peace and prosperity forever. Hoping that all the good hearted people will understand my words in the positive light which glows inside them

Today I am sharing my words as a humble request to everyone. Let us all rise from our stressful lives and overcome all the difficulties we face in different forms and shine brightly to spread our own beautiful sunshine of hope and peace to our world! Each one can pass this glow to all who touch your life and together we will overcome this pandemic depression time one day! We can show the future generations by our practices more than our preaching alone. Please "Rise and shine everyday with goodness in your heart and soul"...

Are you strong to help others in adversities or do you need help always?

Yes, we all are humans and we all have our own way of living and thinking. It's a fact that we all are struggling or have struggled at some point or the other in our life. No one and I really mean it that absolutely no one has ever had a life as a bed of roses everyday! Big or small there are hardships and how you handle them makes you a hero or a zero in life!

When you take one step upwards in life with your success you will realise how powerful you have become. But when you turn towards a weaker person to help him rise above his adverse situation you become more powerful and that's when you become a true hero. I really adore those people who practice good works and do charity in spite of struggling in their own life. They don't just inspire but literally prespire to inspire me more and teach me what is true heroism and goodness of heart! I know this is very hard to do myself but I want to try to be as good as these heroes so that one day someone gets inspired by poor me too!

Seriously a big salute of respect to all our real life heroes who inspire us to beat the demons of failure harder and emerge as better humans in life...Stay happy and blessed always.

#success #people #charity #respect #help #salute

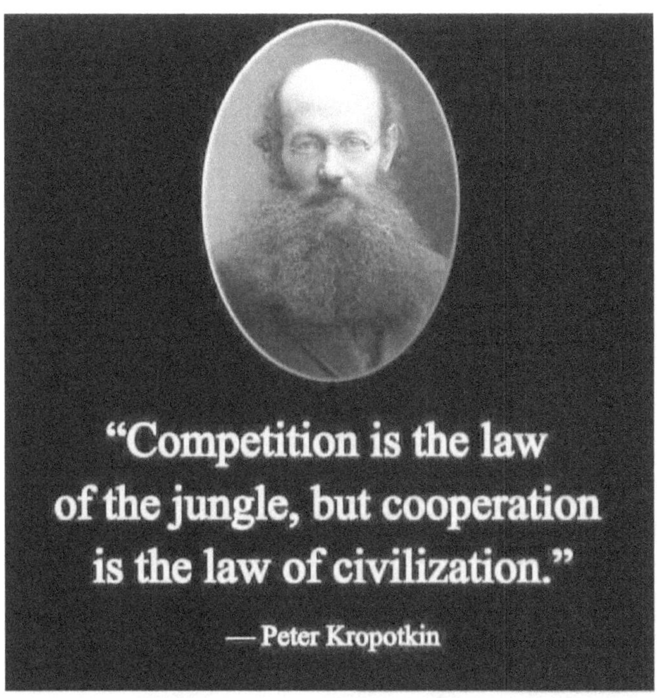

Does peace and harmony bring happiness in life and in your works?

I know you must be thinking that winning any competition and becoming the best and most rich is the most common idea of being a successful person in the world today. Then how can peace and harmony make you happy and successful? But I request you to imagine a world where you are so rich that you have all the money, luxuries and comforts that it can buy but you are alone in this state...How much can you enjoy and for how long can you enjoy this blissful state?

After a point of time you will my dear readers truly long for people as family and friends to be with you and together enjoy all these super comforts. For that to happen you have bring peace and harmony in all your relationships both professionally and personally. The beautiful balance that both peace and harmony bring in you and in all your life's endeavors will make you truly happy forever. This is the wonderful legacy you can pass on to your next generation and these values are truly unbeatable in comparison to any other riches of the world.

If you have good health and a healthy family to support you with love then that's the treasure of peace. Is there anything more valuable than this peace which makes your body and soul feel invincible and truly rich with abundant happiness? Please choose your peace and create harmony in all your relationships and endeavors in life. This will make our civilisation the best civilisation in human history. Thanks for understanding my humble thoughts and for your patience too to understand this deep thought. Stay happy and blessed always.

#business #health #people #happiness #love #money

Do you smile and speak with good manners to all? Yes, we all are educated and are coming from good families but have you ever wondered why there are so many conflicts happening in spite of this back up of knowledge and moral values ?

It's a simple and very much neglected issue...Yes it's the tone in which you are having your conversation. Sometimes there is no eye contact, no smile and no extra words of Welcome and Thanks....That's when many egos are hurt and with this aggressive attitude small matters blow out of proportion and create rifts, misunderstandings and even unwanted separations...

Please think and react with a little more sweetness to

others. Would you like to see a smile then please smile yourself too! You look awesome when you smile and speak softly! I am sure this will reflect on the other person's face too. So half the battle is won and there will be so much peace that you will not need to fight the second battle at all!

So please stay happy and spread your happiness with every human you interact and see the magic of peace overpower you everyday. Thank you and wishing you all happiness in all your endeavors in life.

#thankyou #happiness #react #like

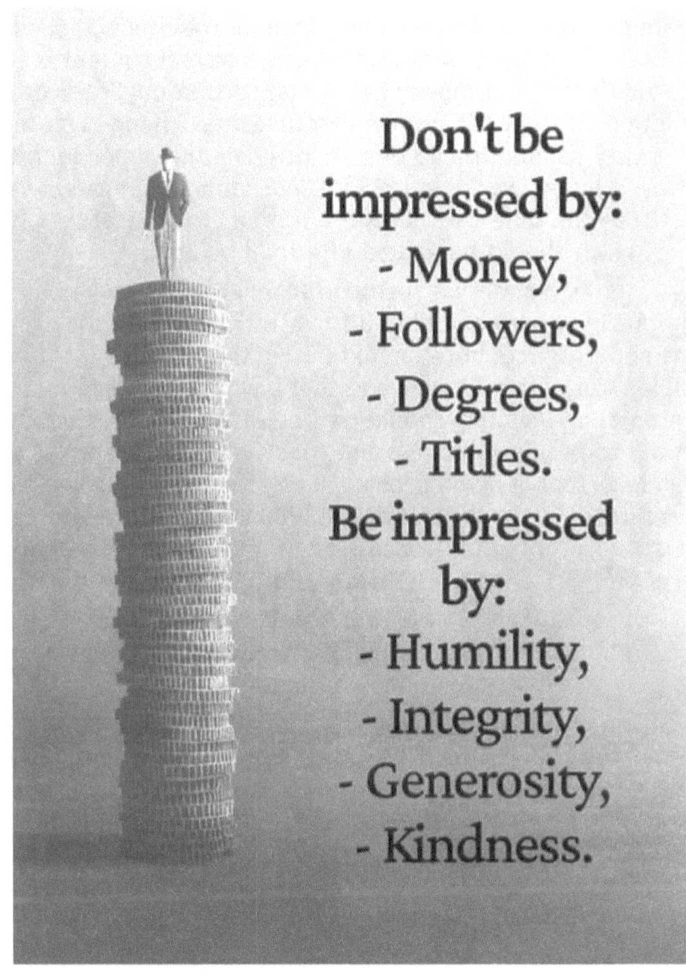

First impressions are the best impressions but are they the real truth or just an outer shine to create wrong impressions?

Yes! today the whole marketing strategy which we see makes humans look like all perfect. Many brands use celebrities, just with this profit making intention, for selling their products to their target audience. Public Relations experts turn simple products and services into great unbelievable works which deflates like a balloon when the consumer experiences the harsh truth. You are paying more for the brand than for the product. Similarly the outer image is given so much focus that real content is completely different and mostly below standard in quality. Even the marketing strategy for human resources has changed so much that a very pseudo image of ever positive and super human is portrayed to the world which actually is done by image building experts. By the time one learns the truth its too late and the true values which should be valued lose their value....

Its high time we focus on highlighting true values like good quality, greater utility and relatively sensible pricing. Humans and products both should be endurable, sustainable and reliable. Truth lasts forever and that's why the real foundation for promoting anything should be true quality and best content. That will add to the goodness and goodwill of your brands to such a high level that you will become successful in your business and life. All the younger generations will follow the ethical and rational path to attain great success so that the older generation is always proud of them. Stay happy and successful always.

#qualitymatters #brand #content #sustainable
#humanresources #building #marketingstrategy
#publicrelations #business #success

Are you tired of proving your views to be right to others?

The real cause of stress many times is seen to be a lack of understanding one another especially when you feel highly undervalued, misunderstood and ignored by those whom you think should have understood you in your life. You feel betrayed and are hurt and many people end up living sadly in permanent loneliness and solitude due to suffering from these factors.

Just to know more about how even you can be wrong in some situations I request you to please close your eyes and put yourself in the other person's place. Now rewind the time and play that incident how it happened..You will understand that you were wrong and that other person was right and he or she never intended any hurt on you. They wanted your best and were explaining only that to you so they had to point out your mistakes. Yes my friend you will never learn or grow wiser in life if you are not corrected in time by someone who actually cares for you. Being right for one can be and will be wrong for someone else and that's life. No two humans are the same and everyone has their own thought and viewpoint.

But if you realise your mistakes and correct your feelings and your actions in time only then you will emerge as a true champion in your life. So please be kind to yourself and others by trying to judge your feelings impartially to learn and grow from your mistakes. Thank you for your sweet patience for my humble words..Stay happy and blessed always.

#people #building #team

Relationships #Peace #Unity #intergrity

Please 'Express' your appreciation more to all people who touch your lives. One simple word of gratitude like 'Thanks' or the simplest praise like 'You are Awesome' hardly takes a few seconds of your precious time. But the impact of these sweet words remain with that other person for the whole day. Sometimes one simple sentence like " I UNDERSTAND how hard it is for you" which reflects your empathetic and understanding attitude can save difficult relationships from breaking apart. So my dear readers please make your life beautiful by spreading your beautiful smile with sweet words of gratitude, appreciation and become angels on earth. Thank you for your patience and understanding for reading my words till the end. Stay happy and blessed always.

#happinessmatters #gratitude #peacebuilding

Self respect and dignity is very important in life so I request all of you to please maintain that golden quality in your life both professionally and personally. You are the creator of your own happiness and peace which requires you to fight all the odds that you face as major obstacles in your life's journey. Try to remain calm and ignore those people who threaten your peace in any way. Smile strongly and remain silent on matters which make you angry and at places where you cannot respond as badly as you want in your inner self. Nothing hurts a negative person more than your big and sweet 'Smile' and your not getting disturbed by their actions! Your power increases and their power finishes...so please stay strong always as you are strong deep inside your soul. Please try to have a warrior spirit with the Angelic calmness to guard your dignity and self respect in all your relationships in life...Thank you all.

#people #thankyou #quality #power #happiness #respect

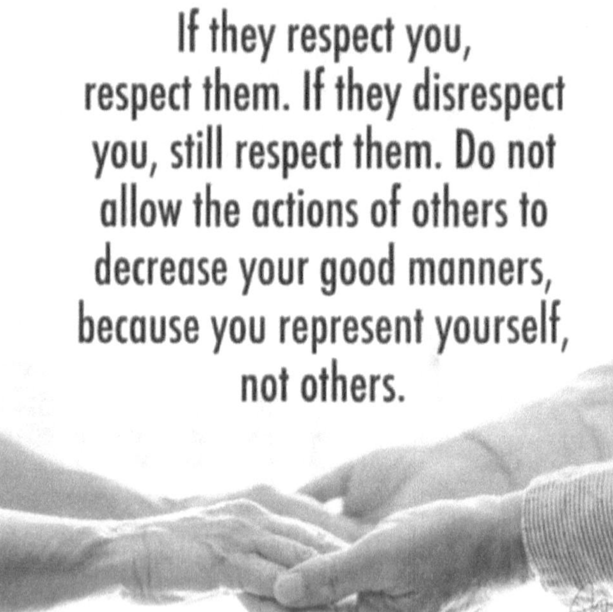

Empathy is the best part of a human heart. Sympathy for all humans and animals is a golden virtue of a great soul.... We all have problems in life and life is never a bed of roses for every one all the time. If you can understand another person's struggles and help them with empathy and sympathy then you become like a sweet angel like friend to them. Please stop judging and passing comments without understanding others. Don't we all want good friends who understand and support us during our crisis times and not just in our happy times?

We all know that lonely people really lead very sad lives especially when you have no one to share your feelings or support you emotionally or financially or morally. I request you all to please show your sweet loving heart to those who need it especially in these critical highly stressful times where everyone is facing difficulties which they cannot discuss with others most of the times due to many reasons. Your sweet smile, your kind words, your generous support and some of your precious time is all that it takes to spread this invaluable joy to them. If each of us spread such happiness to all whom we meet in our lives then I am sure this world would become like a beautiful paradise very soon... Stay happy and blessed always..God bless you.

#empathymatters #happiness #Sympathy
#Peace #teambonding #Harmony

Step forward with a bold spirit and you will emerge as a strong and successful hero surely! Yes I understand that there are moments when you will doubt your self..as whether you are right or if you will do well or what others will say if you commit a mistake! But deep within your heart please say 'I can and I will' and 'I will win this one for sure'...and then definitely you will be a winner! Stay happy and confident always.

Confidence # Beat the fears #successmindset

Life teaches you many lessons and the biggest lesson var-
ies according to your priorities and the rewards you achieve in
your life. A positive and optimistic attitude can work wonders for
you and make you happily overcome many negative circumstances successfully. Experience this positive attitude and you
will vote for its truth surely. Stay happy and positive always.

#work #experience #positiveenergy #happiness

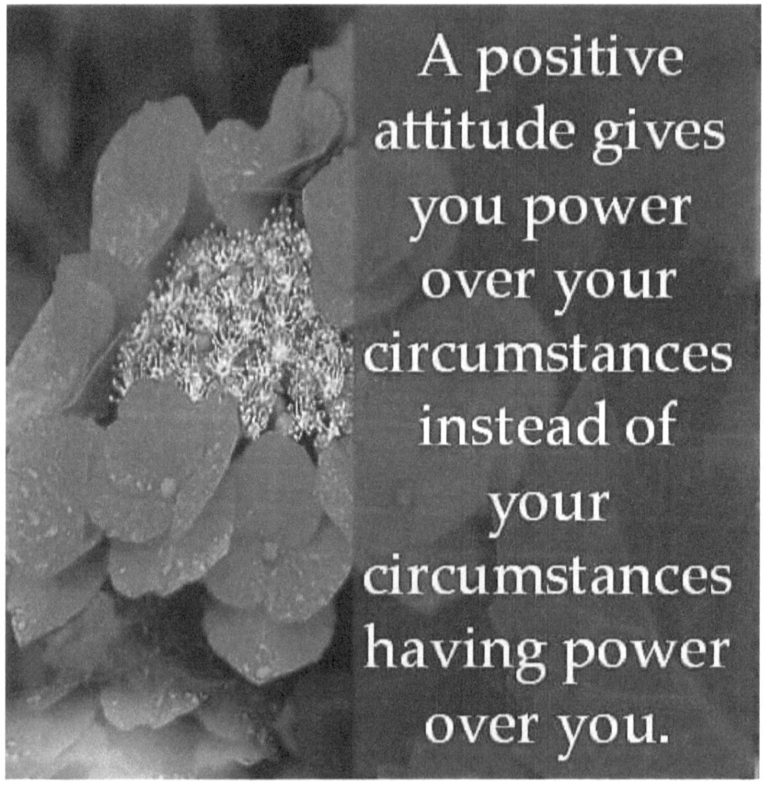

— Warren Buffett —

"An idiot with a plan can beat a genius without a plan."

— Talk-to Mastermind —

Time and Tide wait for none. If you really to want to succeed beautifully in life you must have a very sensible and brilliant plan of action always. Ensure you follow this smart plan and eventually victory will be yours always.

> "Go wisely and slowly.
> Those who rush
> stumble and fall."

— Talk-to Mastermind—

If you practice patience in the understanding of each step or stage of your life then you will enjoy and learn more to become mature and wiser in the process. Do you agree with these wise words of William Shakespeare? Try to ponder upon these and answer whatever you feel...Thanks for your patience for me to read and think till here...Stay happy and blessed always 🤍🙏

Patience #peacebuilding # Success# Happiness #success

Successful people never run away from hardships to attain their goals in life. We can see even Bees and Ants work so hard everyday to fulfill their goals.Hardwork, dedication and perseverance are the trisome weapons to be used by a strong warrior who wants to be successful by beating all fears or stumble blocks and conquer the real victory in life's battles...Stay happy and strong in all your endeavors in life.

#work #people #Motivation #Leadership skills

You cannot pour from an empty pot...Can you? Yes so to give you must have something in you good enough ...Yes you have to take care of yourself first. I know some philosophers will call me selfish and I really don't mind that...Until you are strong enough how can you strengthen anything or anyone else. A mother who is strong can take excellent care for her children but if she cannot even stand straight, how can you blame her for her failures as a mother...This is just an example...Please grow stronger first in every way and then help others...even a money plant grows beautifully when it's tied to a strong tree! Stay happy and blessed always.

#help #eachforequal
Empowerment # Motivation #motivation

> **If you can look at problems as temporary setbacks and stepping-stones to success, you will come to believe that the only limitations you have are the ones in your own mind.**

Treat your problems like challenges and learn to beat your fears everyday. This can be done by making sure that you are very strong in your mind. No hurdles are too big or impossible to cross as long as you have a strong spirit in your heart and soul. Stay strong and successful with a sweet smile of confidence each day.You are your own hero and you will win every challenge life throws at you.

#motivation #Perseverance #Success #bravehearts

Face your fears to beat them fearlessly. Yes, first step to lead a brave and truly happy life is to beat your fears and that is an endless process which is why life teaches you the best lessons. Life has enough battles for those who live with passion and purpose. Yes, the winners are those only who fight them with wisdom and vigour. But to do that you have to first identify what's your fear or that factor which is acting as your biggest barrier. Once you face that fact or truth, you can with your strong will power and dedication filled with perseverance, kill that horrible fear forever! So please be strong, and stay alert of all those fears which are stopping your feet from stepping forward in life. Hope that you all can become happy and truly positive in winning this battle against all your fears. Thanks for being human and please stay calm and happy always.

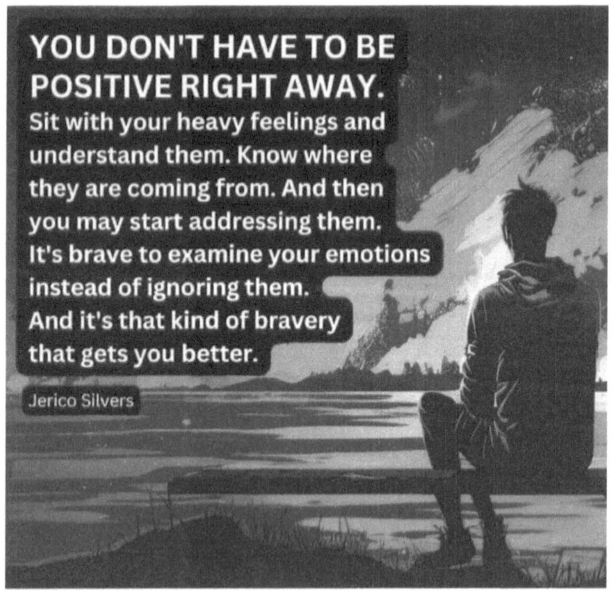

You can never win playing dirty.
Karma is real.
You reap what you sow.
What goes around comes around.

We all want success and happiness in life. There are all kinds of people in this big and beautiful world. The good hearted and hardworking people will always be prosperous which is the blessing they get for leading a peaceful life. But there are people who play dirty to get easy gains by pulling down good and successful people. They are the manipulators who use venomous ways to spread hatred and cause failure especially for the good hearted humans. Please stay away from such evil minded people as they are very dangerous and only can add to misery of others. By taking revenge you are only wasting your precious peace and spoiling your health, so please first let go. Then let their Karma or actions will give them the punishment they deserve definitely one day. So please stay happy, peaceful and reflect good health in every way. Thank you for reading my thoughts and understanding me. Stay happy and blessed always.

#success #health #thankyou #people #happiness

Fighting depression

Have you ever wondered why people are always judging others more rather than accepting them just as they are? Do we know what they are suffering? Some people love to pass judgments on others based on superficial factors. ...Let's take a small pause and be kind to all our fellow humans and break all the barriers which make us judge more and love less... You are born to be the best and by becoming more kind you actually become the best! Please stay happy and kind always.

#people #hope #kindness #Happiness

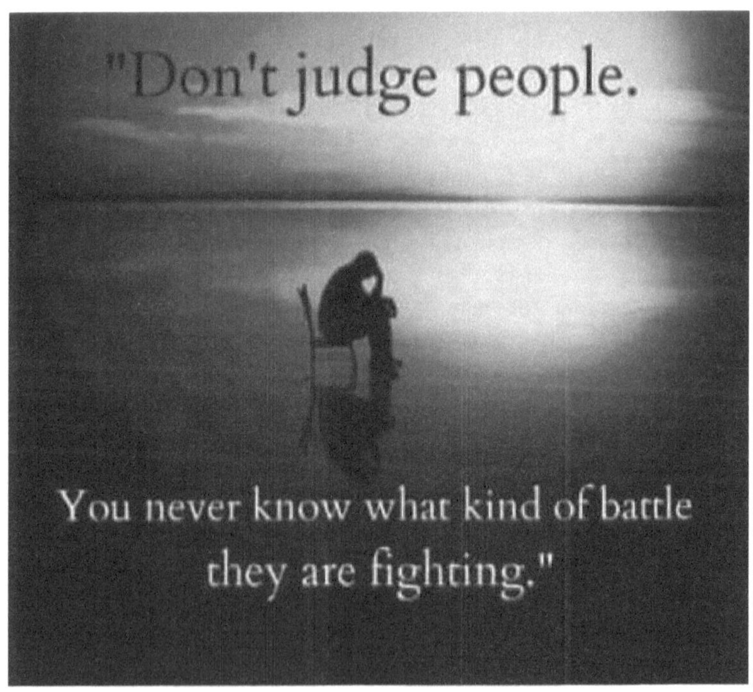

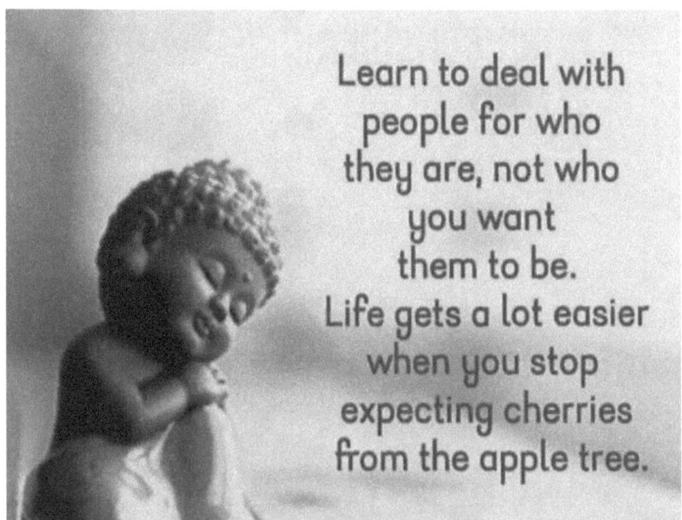

Why do you get angry with someone? Is it when they do not exactly behave the way you want them to? or does someone who always disobeys your orders make you angry beyond all limits? Yes, I can understand when this happens with adults especially in work places especially if you are the boss and all others should obey your commands. But if you ever pause and try to find the exact reason behind this defiance and rude disobedience then with an empathetic heart you will forgive this person. Imagine if this person is your own child who is suffering or your own family member who is facing many health or emotional problems which they cannot share with you....Does your heart feel that I should have been more kind to him now? If yes then please show that kindness by your words and actions so that the innocent sufferer feels good, and then you will see the difference in that same person's attitude towards you. A little smile and a listening heart with some patience and without very high expectations can really transform your anger and hatred. You will feel lighter and better and that feeling will grow with time slowly making you the Best Boss and the Best Human being..Thanks for showing your patience for reading till here for me. Stay happy, peaceful and truly blessed always.

#health #work #kindness #share

Provoking people beyond their limits is one of the main strategies in marketing and advertising. Yes.. many times these persuasive influences can actually bring out the beast in you rather than enhance the beauty in you! Do you agree that pressures to succeed in your unreasonable targets can drive the beast in you to pounce at others? Calm attitude is what all philosophical doctrines preach but how long does one control the demons inside a highly stressful mind? Ignoring the adversaries and embracing the peace is a big mission which one should undertake to succeed happily in all our works both personally and professionally. Kindness is undoubtedly a very beautiful value to practice more than just preaching. So please guard yourself to achieve all the peace and happiness you truly deserve in life. Stay happy and blessed always.

#marketing # persuasion #peacebuilding
#leadership # Stress Management # Strength

Patience and perseverance are two strong values which together can make you into the most successful human and you will excel in any role you play in your life. The best way to learn your skills is with best education and rigorous training. To become the best you should know the best and practice that best in action by becoming that better each time. Best things are surely going to happen to such people especially when they never give up on themselves in life. Do you agree? I hope and pray all of you who are reading this for motivating yourself will definitely grow wiser and become successful in life. Thank you and wishing you all the best in life always joy

#education #training #thankyou #people

#motivation #Goodness

I believe that you should smile more whenever someone wants to see you cry. That is the best way to show how strong you are and nothing hurts your enemies more than that! The best revenge is to ignore your rivals and move forward in life with a vengeance to be happy always! You are your master and you are the 'Real winner' if you are stronger and more confident than your haters...So walk ahead in life with your head held high and do the best all your endeavors in life with a big smile! Fortune indeed favours the brave.

Beat your fears # Motivation #Happiness

Do you have any goal which seems impossible to achieve?

Yes, life is a journey where we have different goals at different stages. Some we easily accomplish but there are some for which we have to work double and wait double for its accomplishment. If you are brave, you will take it as a challenge and work with full spirit of determination to achieve this goal. Your dedication, determination and perseverance will lead you to fulfill this goal definitely one day! So never stop dreaming and most important never ever stop working for fulfilling your goals no matter what you suffer....Stay focused and you will make the impossible possible one day for sure! You have the spark deep inside you and that will ignite with your hardwork, dedication and perseverance to make you truly and happily successful one day.

#successmindset

#work # Motivation # Hope #positivity

Leaders lead the path as we all see but is Leadership an easy path?

To be a leader needs many qualities especially if your team has to successful in all its endeavors. The Motivation strategy in which the leader promotes each team member to do his best is the most important step. To lead as an example should take the leader work hard both in action and words.Its easy to wear the crown but as we heard in the Spiderman movies with great power comes great responsibility! So are you a leader or a follower is your choice but to excel in Leadership means you have great responsibility with the backbone of great power! Do you agree or disagree?

#leadership #team #leaders #work

#motivation #strategy #leader #power

Magic of your spoken words is unimaginable!

We all are always scolded by our family or teachers when we speak anything which hurts others. But have you ever thought that the magic of your speech can actually be used to inspire others to do the impossible! Yes, your words have the power to create and destroy others lives! Let's us ponder on these words to get the key to this magic...

When you think positively you reflect that positivity to others whoever comes in close conversations with you. You become the ultimate motivator as a friend or family member or even in your workplace you can become the motivation that many people desperately need in these stressful times. The opposite happens when you are brooding and cribbing in negativity. You become a curse on others and am sure that once they realise that they will run away from you! So my dear readers the choices is yours and the best choice is to use the power of your words for spreading peace, hope and motivation always! Thank you for understanding and hope you use your magical words for uplifting all the people you touch in your life! Spread your magic through your words in all ways!

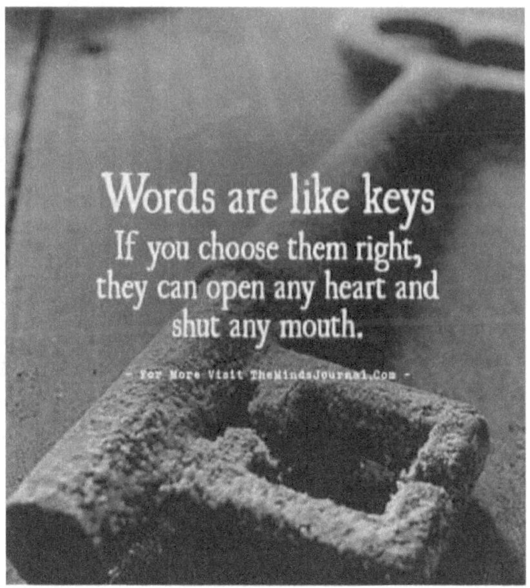

FORGIVENESS IS A VIRTUE OF THE BRAVE.

Indira Gandhi

Brave who forgave...

October 31st 1984 was a big date in the Indian history which marks the death anniversary of the Indian Prime Minister Mrs Indira Gandhi. The assassination created sensation but the ripples of this are still felt in the hearts of many Indians. I am not talking about politics here as that can be and has been twisted and tilted by many to favour or disown many and for too long now. I am talking about a golden virtue called Forgiveness which is truly the need and only breed which should last for bringing peace in humanity.

Indira Gandhi had said, "Forgiveness is the virtue of the brave" Does this mean that if someone kills or hurts you or your loved ones you should forgive them? Can such big heart exist in reality or is it only for saints and preachers? Jesus said if you forgive others then you will be forgiven by God. In fact many religions and spiritual teachings world over have been teaching this noble virtue for so many years.

It is very difficult to forgive and even more difficult to stay in hatred without forgiving. Actually by forgiving you are setting yourself free from the chains of hatred and frustration! Fortune indeed favours the brave and if you are brave enough to forgive you are liberating yourself from unending suffering and misery. When you show a forgiving heart you are saving your relationship and your dignity. You become richer in peace and this joy is eternal. Holding on to hatred without letting go will harm you in the long and short run. As wars will end the world but for peace, forgiveness is the only way !

Be brave and forgive before you hit the grave and end life in regrets and misery. You live only once and no one knows how long so being happy and peaceful is more important than brooding in grief! That's the best legacy you can give your present and future generations...

The world needs peace and harmony and we all can take steps in solidarity to sustain this together.

Be brave and forgive more for peace and harmony!

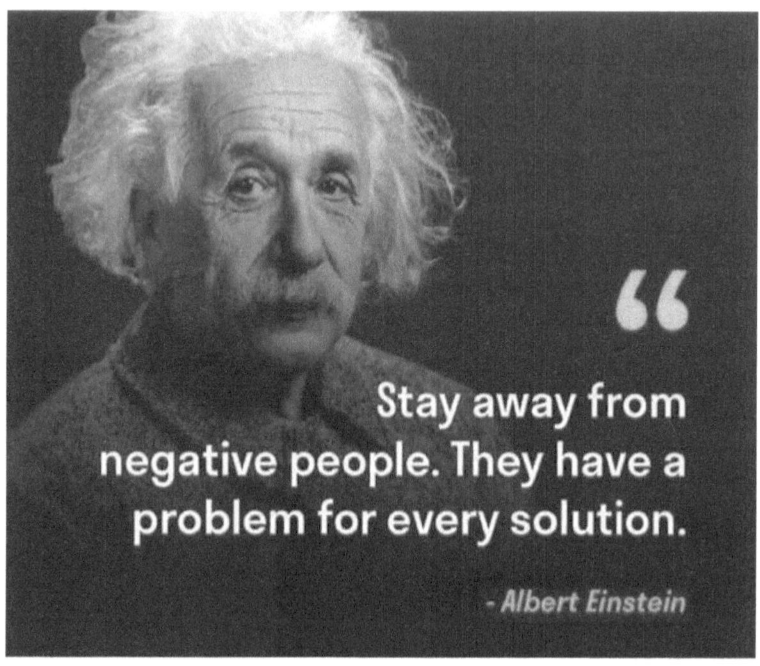

Rise and Shine to Win

Darkness in minds leads to darkness in life. Yes! We all face negative circumstances and people in life. But to win in adverse situations we must stick hard to the positive ray of light. You can and you will rise from negativity and shine with positivity if you choose this path to win. It's a matter of choice and life is about making the right choices. Albert Einstein once said that, "Stay away from negative people. They have a problem for every solution." How true are these words even today. There are negative people in almost all walks of life but if you stay strong not to get discouraged you are already a winner.

Dalai Lama once said do not let the bad behaviour of others affect the inner peace of your soul. There will be always opposition in some form but how you tackle this makes you the real hero. We all are survivors in this post covid era and these experiences have taught us so many life lessons. Personally and professionally I am sure every human has been affected in some way or the other. The stress and anxiety levels have risen beyond limits and infiltrated lives at all places and in all ages. So we need to focus more on rising against this tide before it takes us all down forever.

I am coming back to Einstein's another quote which says that, "You never fail until you stop trying."

First we must make ourselves strong and then pass on this strength to our family and friends. Slowly and steadily this chain reaction will trigger positivity and happiness to all humans around the globe. Together we all can rise and shine to win the race in this life. So smile please and spread the shine always!

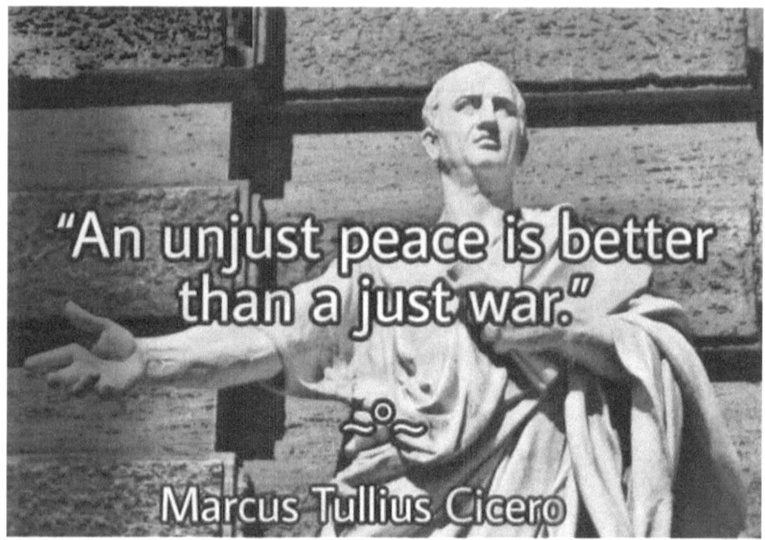

"Peace is universal prosperity"

We are facing turbulent times in the world where war for good health was being won slowly but war for power overtook this to bring doom again in various forms. The Covid giant had taught so many lessons to mankind but the vicious python of power seems to overpower this with its deadly bite.

Where there is no good health in the mind or body there is no prosperity or joy. Peace is the real foundation to build up nations and treasures of happiness for everyone globally. Just reasons to kill are not needed but just reasons to live are a necessity which is the moral and ethical duty of everyone as a part of mankind. Let's pray for peace and harmony and work towards prosperity hand in hand to give our future generations a happy world to live peacefully. May Peace and Prosperity prevail in abundance on you and your families always.

Never let any failure break you and only let it teach you the big lesson to move forward more strongly towards the way for your bigger success one day...as you are a strong warrior in front of the challenges in life.Your determination and dedication will help you achieve your success in life, so stay strong and never give up your dreams!

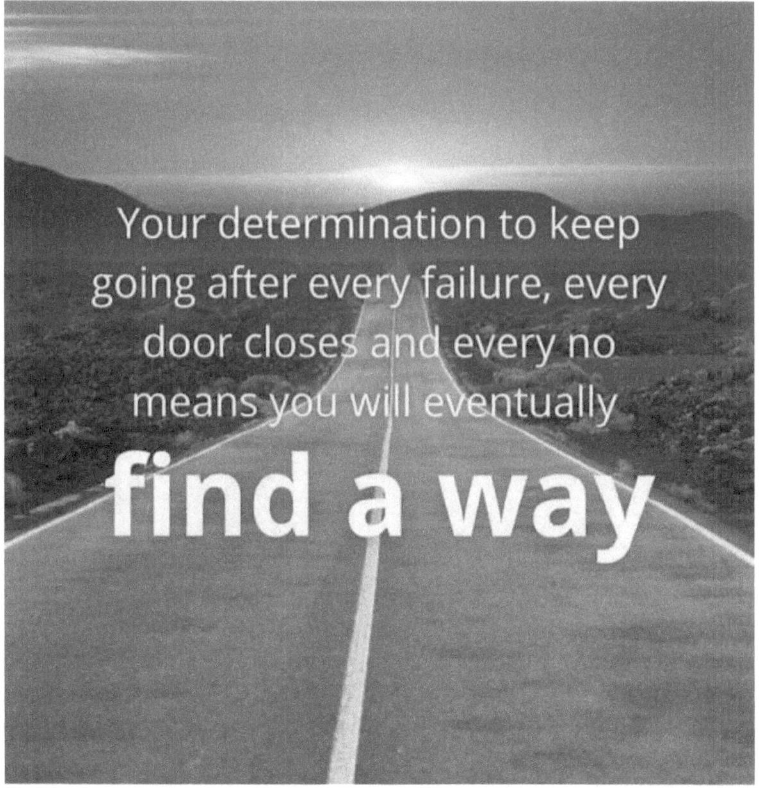

Optimism is the stepping stone which leads you to hope and confidence needed to overcome the challenges life loves to throw at you..So please try to stay happy and strong to spread your sunshine for yourself and all those who look up to you for hope in life! You live only once and that's the reason for living life fully without regrets....

Peace and harmony is true happiness! Wherever you are and however well you do in life if you don't have peace of mind and harmony in your relationships you can never be truly happy for a long time. Life is the biggest teacher and experience is the biggest lesson which only you can learn by living each day. Hardships make you stronger to face life if you take them as challenges so let's make these hardships our stepping stones to happiness. To fret, cry, and get depressed is human but to emerge from these ashes towards peace is divine! Stay peaceful and spread your peace to your family, work fronts and wherever you make an impact as a good hearted human being! Thankfulness and gratitude with the right positive attitude can definitely make your life truly beautiful

You are the Leader

A strong leader makes his followers stronger and his time the strongest in history of a nation. Moral values which have stood the test of time and won battles with wisdom and great endurance are very important in all ages. This truth flows to all nations and all generations...So grow in good spirit for spreading goodness in spirit both as a leader and follower. This will bring true peace and harmony among good hearted humans forever! Thanks for understanding and reading my humble thoughts today..inspired by our Father of the nation Mahatma Gandhi.

We all need to show our kindness and big heart for ourselves and our families both professionally and personally as these critical times demands from us today. If you are the lamp then please glow first bravely and light the way for others to drive away the darkness of depression and suffering! Together we can and together we will overcome this pandemic time too! Thanks for understanding and reading with empathy and integrity

Self respect & Generosity are Your Choices

The world is going through a great crisis but these are golden lessons for a bright future for our coming generations. The attitude to handle any crisis is most important and that needs to be build up wisely to face these challenges. Humans need the basic necessity to survive is the greatest lesson of the 2020 pandemic time. But to live our breath for survival we need to let others also live and breathe. We are all hearing and seeing many generous actions of our noble fellow humans globally. But there are the thorns of misusers and evil minded venomous humans who hurt our human roses today. Let us stay vigilant of all the factors and be wise to overcome this Covid pandemic in the most brilliant way. The judicious use of resources and services is very important along with an emotional love for fellow humans survival today. Let's all make a big chain of positivity, generosity and unity globally to beat this demonic Covid as soon as possible from our mother Earth...Together we can and we will! Hoping and praying for a healthy, happy and prosperous world again with you!

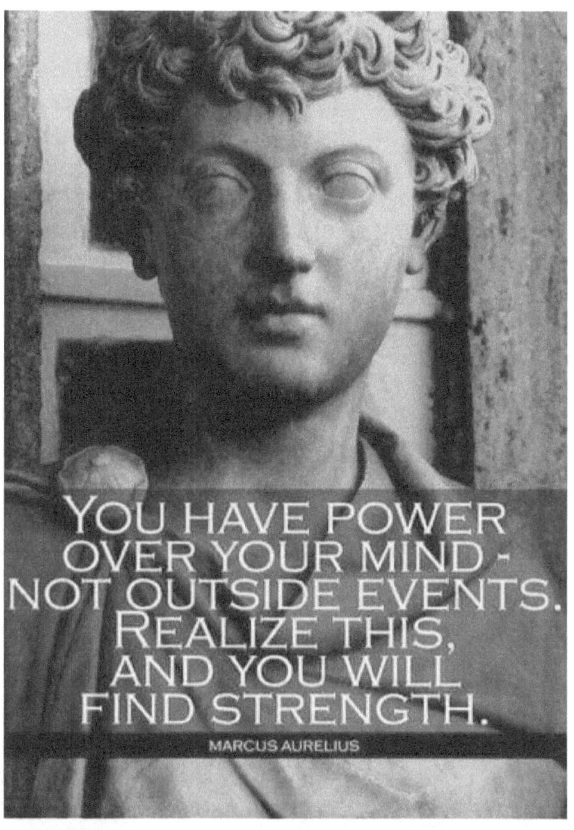

Control over your thoughts leads to control over your actions. Stay strong inside and realise your power to overcome any challenge life throws at you. Uniqueness and intellectual growth comes with time and experience. So please stay strong, blessed and positive come what may in life!

Happiness is a reflection of your thoughts!

We are witnessing a huge global crisis and depression in many spheres worldwide especially after this pandemic time has gripped our world. Let us all try to grow rich in our thoughts by being good to oneself and others so that each person becomes happy and brave enough to face life happily today. We need to think unitedly to become very positive, encouraging and truly empowering so that we all emerge as true warriors and successful winners in life. If each one individual vows to spread their sunshine then we can surely eradicate this darkness of depression from our families and our society one day. Let this light spread as sweet sunshine through our thoughts to others. We should empower and overcome our fears strongly so that our generations both younger and elder can come out of this emotional turmoil. We all can help others and make a strong chain of human efforts towards achieving this sweet world in reality. Wishing everyone a strong, positive and happy life ahead.

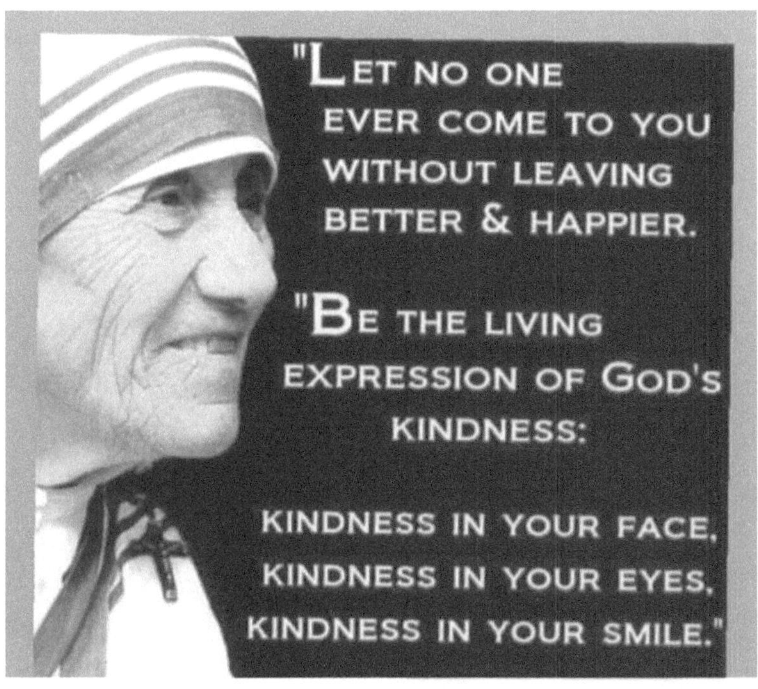

Please try to be good and kind to everyone you meet in your life. You will never know all the personal battles each human is fighting inside their hearts and souls which they hide with a superficial smile for the world for many reasons. One smile, one kind compliment and one sweet word of gratitude is enough for you to look and feel truly beautiful so please do this simply each day. You will feel beautiful and amazed at how much love, hope and peace you can spread gradually which will make you the glowing Sun or Surya with sweet warm sunshine for all your family, friends, well wishers and strangers. These positive vibes will spread happiness and peace wherever you go and reflect in great blessings for you forever! Thanks for understanding and patiently reading my humble words...Stay happy and blessed always